A DREAM OF PASSION

A Dream of Passion is Strasberg's journey of discovery that led to the Method. It begins with an account of his own experiences as a young actor. Strasberg describes his excitement attending performances by the Moscow Art Theatre under Stanislavsky's direction and analyses how Stanislavsky began to solve the central problem of all actors, how to perform night after night with the same degree of energy and inspiration.

Strasberg shows how Stanislavsky's system was applied and adapted through work with the Group Theatre and later at the Actors Studio. The result was the Method, a controversial approach to acting which has helped some of the finest performers on the American stage. By analysing performances by key actors Strasberg paints a clear and engrossing portrait of the Method in action. He also demonstrates how the Method can help actors and anyone who is hampered by an inability to express their feelings. *A Dream of Passion* is a work of historic importance for anyone interested in the theatre and the craft of acting.

Lee Strasberg was born in Poland in 1901 and grew up on the Lower East Side of New York. He began his training as an actor at the American Laboratory Theatre in 1923, and in 1931, with Harold Clurman and Cheryl Crawford, he founded the Group Theatre. He directed some of the Group's most famous productions and was in charge of actor training. Strasberg became Artistic Director of the Actors Studio in 1951 and continued to direct on and off Broadway. He also conducted private acting classes at Carnegie Hall and at his own schools, the Lee Strasberg Theatre Institutes. Strasberg resumed his acting career with the role of Hyman Roth in the film *The Godfather, Part II* in 1974. He died in 1982.

A DREAM OF
PASSION

THE DEVELOPMENT OF
THE METHOD

LEE STRASBERG

Edited by Evangeline Morphos

Methuen Drama

First published in Great Britain in 1988
by Bloomsbury Publishing Limited.
Published in this paperback edition in 1989
by Methuen Drama
an imprint of Reed Consumer Books Limited
Michelin House, 81 Fulham Road, London SW3 6RB
and Auckland, Melbourne, Singapore and Toronto

Reprinted 1992

British Library Cataloguing in Publication Data

Strasberg, Lee, *1901–1982*
    A dream of passion: the development of the method
    1. Theatre. Acting. Techniques
    I. Title   II. Morphos, Evangeline
    792'.028

ISBN 0-413-19670-4

Printed in Great Britain
by Cox & Wyman Ltd, Reading

FOR ANNA—
THIS BOOK, MY LIFE, MY LOVE
—LEE

Is it not monstrous that this player here,
But in a fiction, in a dream of passion,
Could force his soul so to his own conceit
That from her working all his visage wanned,
Tears in his eyes, distraction in his aspect,
A broken voice, and his whole function suiting
With forms to his conceit? And all for nothing!
For Hecuba!

Hamlet

CONTENTS

PREFACE

IN his original statement of purpose, Lee Strasberg maintained that "this book on acting is intended for a general public. It is not a textbook. It is the first effort by anyone to explain, what is acting? What is the Stanislavsky system? What is the Method?" Throughout the time he was writing the book, Strasberg remained adamant that he was writing for an audience interested in the theatre but, more important, for one interested in creativity. In exploring the nature of creativity in the acting process, he sought to draw conclusions about the general nature of the creative process.

Lee Strasberg's original working title for this book was *What Is Acting: From Stanislavsky to the Method*. His intention was to expand on and to explore some of the issues he had already raised in a nine-hundred-word article he had written for the *Encyclopedia Britannica*'s "Acting" entry. (Strasberg's article, in fact, replaced one written by the great actor-director Constantin Stanislavsky.) Strasberg's *Britannica* article ends with a section titled "The Nature of Acting":

> But acting has a history of struggle, progress and development. Acting . . . is the ability to react to imaginary stimuli; and its essential elements remain the twin requisites enunciated by Talma, "unusual sensitivity and extraordinary intelligence," this latter not in the form of book learning but in the ability to comprehend the workings of the human soul. The essential problems in acting — does the actor "feel" or does he merely imitate? should he speak naturally or rhetorically? what is natural? etc. — are as old as acting itself. They derive not from the realistic movement but from the nature of the acting process.

It is the precise "nature of the acting process" that Strasberg explores in this book. This process, according to Strasberg, had long been misunderstood, for two reasons. The first lies in the transitory nature of the art form; the second in the failure to understand the differences between the actor's problem and that of any other artist. Taking a line from Shakespeare, Strasberg described the elusive nature of the acting process in this way:

> . . . the real problem and mystery in acting is that the actor must be able "but in a fiction, in a dream of passion, [to] force his soul so to his own conceit." The exploration of this became the problem of the post-Shakespearean actor.

It was to the discovery of the "mystery" of the acting process that Strasberg devoted his life's work. And it was in Hamlet's speech that he found not only a definition of acting — "a dream of passion" — but the final title of his book.

Lee Strasberg described his life in the theatre as a "voyage," a trip that started out with no fixed destination. He set out to explore the mystery of the process of acting and ended, finally, with the development of the Method. The book traces his voyage through theatrical history, observations of great performances, and his own experiments and discoveries. In effect, it was an adventure of the mind.

As Strasberg saw it, *A Dream of Passion* was to be "the first authentic description of the Method. It describes the way in which the ideas and procedures developed by Stanislavsky were used in the productions of the Group Theatre and the results achieved. It describes additional procedures and exercises discovered to solve some of the problems Stanislavsky had not been able to solve."

Strasberg's process of discovery led finally to an understanding of the nature of creativity. From his discovery of "emotional memory" as a key to the actor's creative process grew his theory that emotional memory is the origin of the creation of any work of art. In this regard, Strasberg stands in a direct line with the great Romantics. Wordsworth described the creation of a work of art (in this case poetry) by describing, in essence, emotional memory:

I have said that poetry is the spontaneous overflow of powerful feelings: it takes its origins from *emotion recollected in tranquillity:* the emotion is contemplated till, by a species of reaction the tranquillity gradually disappears, and an emotion kindred to that which was before the object of contemplation is gradually produced and does itself actually exist in the mind. In this mood successful composition generally begins, and in a mood similar to this it is carried on. (*Strasberg's emphasis*)

Strasberg also felt strongly that the issue of creativity would not only interest the general reader, but that it could be used as a body of knowledge that could enhance anyone's life:

> The final section tries to suggest that the discoveries of Stanislavsky and of the Method as they relate to the creativity of the actor are relevant to the general problem of creativity, which is today a major educational concern.

No doubt, had he lived, Strasberg would have elaborated on these final pages of the book.

Strasberg began work on this book in California in the summer of 1974. At the urging of his wife, Anna, he had begun to record the progress that led to his development of the Method. Working in his study, he dictated a first draft. This accounts for the lively, almost conversational tone that is so much of Strasberg's written style. Often, on the Mondays following his Sunday dictations, he would lecture on the history of theatre to his students at the Lee Strasberg Theatre Institute. The tapes of these lectures reveal that the issues he had just explored were still fresh in his mind. Often, these lectures were used to clarify for himself issues he had just dealt with and thus became the basis for some of his revisions. One lecture is a brilliant analysis of Diderot's famous eighteenth-century essay *The Paradox of Acting;* in another he demonstrates some of the exercises he learned from his acting teacher Richard Boleslavsky.

When Strasberg returned to New York, he continued to work on the manuscript — surrounded by his private collection of thousands of books and theatrical memorabilia. He expanded the section on Boleslavsky, using the notebook he had kept during his time at the American Laboratory Theatre; he included new information on the Group Theatre, using his own notebooks and director's notes; he dealt with Stanislavsky in greater detail; and he added the section on Brecht. Strasberg's own rich collection of historical treatises on acting — many unpublished works or personal letters — fired his work. He also wrote an expanded section on emotional memory as it related to literature and the visual arts. As his work progressed, Strasberg added sections analyzing the work of Grotowski and Artaud.

The manuscript of the book was complete when Lee Strasberg died. What had not been finally determined was the exact order of the sections and the inclusion of the sections he had dictated after the first draft.

I first met Lee Strasberg in the summer of 1981. I had just been appointed Chairman of the Undergraduate Drama Department at New York University's Tisch School of the Arts. Our department is affiliated with the Lee Strasberg Theatre Institute, where our students study acting. Throughout the fall and winter of 1981, I observed a number of Strasberg's classes, attended a series of lectures he gave to his students, and had a number of discussions with him.

After Lee Strasberg died, I organized a year-long tribute to the Group Theatre at the Tisch School. It was at this time that I first read the early draft of this book. Bill Phillips at Little, Brown then asked me to edit the manuscript of the book. Phillips's father, the actor Wendell K. Phillips, had in fact studied with Strasberg. Strasberg felt a very special gratitude for Bill Phillips's belief in the book and his support throughout the writing of it. Bill was patient and understanding after Strasberg's death in respecting Anna Strasberg's wishes to delay publication. He was enormously helpful in guiding the final progress of the book.

As an editor, I felt I had three tasks: to preserve strictly Lee Strasberg's voice and his writings; to clarify the order of the material; and occasionally to clarify sentence structure.

I used the original, dictated manuscript as the foundation for this book, because it seemed to convey his own conversational style best. (He often used "we" or "our" to describe his own work or discoveries because of the collaborative nature of theatre.) To this I added sections from the draft prepared for Little, Brown that included further information on Strasberg's work as a director of the Group Theatre and a section on Bertolt Brecht. These were very important points to Strasberg. In his original statement of purpose, he talked about the need to "help define the style of the Group Theatre productions as being somewhat different from the conventional idea of realism and to show how the Group Theatre contributed to the production style for the future — including even an influence on the theatre of Brecht about which hitherto unavailable material is advanced."

Strasberg had dictated separately, but had not located it finally in the manuscript, a discussion of the relationship of emotional memory to the other arts. He had again raised the examples of Wordsworth and Proust that he had used in his *Encyclopedia Britannica* article. This section I placed after Strasberg's discussion of emotional memory.

Strasberg had written that "there is no need for illustrations. But, if thought advisable, interesting illustrations of great actors . . . could be included." I have used portraits and memorabilia of some of the great actors discussed in the book, as well as photos of Strasberg himself. All of this material is drawn from his private collection.

Lee Strasberg had said he was "psychologically incapable" of writing an autobiography, and in this book he mentions incidents from his own life only as they relate to his discoveries. The reader might find it helpful to have a brief outline of his life.

Strasberg was born in 1901 in Budzanow, Poland, came to the U.S. in 1909, and grew up in the immigrant neighborhood of the Lower East Side in New York. This culturally rich community was where he first encountered theatre. In 1923 he began his training as an actor at the American Laboratory Theatre, run by Richard Boleslavsky. In 1931, with Harold Clurman and Cheryl Crawford, Strasberg founded the Group Theatre. Its aim was to form a company of actors who produced plays as well as to develop a systematic approach to actor training based on the work of Stanislavsky. Lee Strasberg not only directed the first plays of the Group Theatre but was in charge of the actor training. It was here that he began to develop his system of actor training, the Method. Strasberg left the Group Theatre in 1936 to pursue his directing career independently. When he became Artistic Director of the Actors Studio in 1951, Strasberg's work was firmly implanted as the dominant influence on American acting.

He continued to direct on Broadway and off, and conducted private classes in addition to his work at the Actors Studio. He also founded the Lee Strasberg Theatre Institutes in New York and Los Angeles, which continue his work today. In 1974, with *The Godfather, Part II*, Strasberg resumed his career as an actor — this time in film.

Lee Strasberg died of a heart attack on February 17, 1982, in New York, leaving behind a permanent legacy in the theatre.

Evangeline Morphos
New York
April 1987

A DREAM OF
PASSION

INTRODUCTION

ɴ January 1937, the popular and well-respected theatre
and film personality Walter Huston starred in a Broadway
production of *Othello*. It was a fiasco. As is sometimes the
case in commercial theatre, no one knew exactly why.
Some critics said one thing, others the opposite; some
spectators were dissatisfied with one element, others with a
very different one. The producers were in a frenzy, not
knowing where to fix the blame.

Huston wrote a bittersweet anecdotal piece about this
experience that appeared in the March 1937 issue of the
glamorous *Stage Magazine*. It was entitled "In and Out of
the Bag: Othello Sits Up in Bed the Morning After and
Takes Notice." Although Huston intended to write a
humorous article about performing a classical play on the
commercial stage, he inadvertently touched upon an age-
old topic that related to the special artistic problem of the
actor. He stated that he had been particularly elated the
opening night "by the stimulation of a large New York first
night audience, which always brings a great excitement to

bestow upon the play if the actor will absorb it." Huston had never felt better. He had really enjoyed himself. The actors had the feeling that the audience was responding: they could sense it on the stage; they felt they had the audience in the palms of their hands. They were certain that the production was a success. "We earnestly believed, as deep down as a man can, that we had given a hell of a performance, as fine a piece of work as our lives ever fashioned."

When Huston awoke the next morning, despite every actor's reluctance to read the reviews, he picked up the *Daily News* first because he knew Burns Mantle's star system of rating could be seen at a glance. The mild two-and-a-half stars gave him quite a shock. He hastily opened the *New York Times*, looking for Brooks Atkinson's highly regarded opinion, only to find that this was no more favorable than Mantle's. Throughout the day, Huston grappled with the other reviews as they appeared. But the results were always negative. Huston describes his surprise and confusion over the critical response:

> I could hardly believe it. After all those months of work, after all that fond care, after all that had been said, after hundreds of changes and experiments — after we had patted down every minute detail, could it be that we had produced such a poor thing?
>
> The brunt of all the criticism fell on me. No matter how I deluded myself, I could not escape the clear cry against my performance. I tried to tell myself that the trouble with the critics was that they did not want me, whom they considered a homespun fellow, to try to put on airs. I refused to see any truth in the adverse criticism I read, but instead turned it around and used it to criticize the critics. Did they know that I had studied the role longer, had given it more thought

than any role I had ever played? Couldn't they accept my conception rather than dictate to me from their ignorance? But then I knew this argument would not hold water either. All they knew about my performance, I was slow to admit, was that it did not move them; that it did not grasp and hold their interest; that it did not entertain them, did not ring their approbative bells. On the contrary, their stomachs ached for me. But then I knew that even if I had encompassed the character of the Einstein Theory so that it made plain and good sense to me, it need not necessarily therefore appeal to the public. That was a hard and large lump to swallow.

Huston's experience was not a new one. In fact, his questions — which he saw in personal rather than theatrical terms — predate his Broadway *Othello* by more than 2,000 years. They are manifestations of the essential problem of the actor. For Huston, the issues were simple and direct: How was it possible for an actor to feel that he had accomplished a truthful and dynamic characterization, only to discover the critics in complete disagreement with him? One could reformulate Huston's bewildered inquiries into the problematic relationship between the actor's thought and feeling and his expressive form. But Huston's questions point to an even larger problem: How is great acting produced?

We have had instances of great acting and great actors, but few accounts from either the performers themselves or their critics as to how such greatness was achieved or of the procedures necessary to create or recreate it. Before the discoveries of the great Russian director Constantin Stanislavsky, all acting was thought to be either inspirational or external. Now we know of a third approach.

This book is an attempt to put together many kinds of

information that explain this third approach — what is commonly called "the Method." The Method is really a continuation of and an addition to Stanislavsky's system in Russia. I have tried to assemble these materials in the sequence that I experienced or discovered them so that the reader may understand the Method's development as I became aware of the actor's problem and its solution. Looking back at the unfolding of my career — from spectator to actor to director to teacher to theoretician — I have thought of my life not as a preplanned journey, but rather an open-ended and fortuitous voyage. And in some ways, the discovery of the Method should be viewed in a similar manner.

This voyage begins with my awareness of the central problem of the actor: How can the actor both really feel, and also be in control of what he needs to do on stage? Stanislavsky began to deal with this problem in a systematic way. Our own work at the Group Theatre, at the Actors Studio, and at the Lee Strasberg Theatre Institutes discovered the answers to a second problem: How can the actor make his real feeling expressive on the stage?

THE BEGINNING OF MY VOYAGE
The Search and the Discovery

IT never occurred to me that I would spend my life in the theatre. When I was growing up on New York's Lower East Side after the turn of the century, the professional theatre seemed foreign, far away, something done by other people somewhere else. At an age when young actors normally pose in front of bedroom mirrors before the wild accolades of an imaginary audience, I was reading books and dreaming of ancient history, of warring cradles of civilization, of military commanders with impossible-sounding names. If someone were to have told my parents at that time that I would develop into a Broadway director, Hollywood actor, or head of world-renowned acting institutes, they would have just smiled at me and shrugged. There was no indication in my behavior, no secret background, no stage- and star-struck relatives, no lightning stimulus that would lead one — least of all me — to think that I would be involved with some of the most important innovations in acting and the making of theatre. But fate sometimes works quite otherwise than we expect.

If my childhood environment was without glamour — even the fictionalized kind that Hollywood likes to portray as pre–World War I, poverty row — the Lower East Side did percolate with enthusiasm, with a deep and even obsessive thirst for knowledge and culture. My brother-in-law, Max Lippa, was a salesman who traveled around the country buying old jewelry from which he extracted the gold. Yet this simple need to earn a living was not sufficient for people at that time. There was a strong cultural incentive everywhere. Max became a member of a group called the Progressive Dramatic Club.

My brother-in-law did not do much acting, but he had the makings of a brilliant makeup artist. I would watch with amazement while he created different makeups with crepe hair and paste. I never discovered where and how he had picked up this extraordinary skill.

Every year, in addition to the normal work in the club, he participated in the creation of a huge pageant — usually a celebration of an important Jewish event. The centerpiece of the performance was a historical tableau in which about 150 amateur actors took part. Max created makeup for all these people. He was the one responsible for my first direct contact with the theatre.

The club was about to produce a play in Yiddish by the Austrian playwright Arthur Schnitzler. The play was called *Dos Glick in Winkel;* literally translated it means *A Corner of Happiness.* The club needed an adolescent to play the younger of two brothers. Max recommended me. As an indication of how little concern I had for theatre at that time, I remember neither what the play was about nor the name of the character I played. I know the name of my stage-brother's character only because I can still reexperience the strange and delightful sensation of hearing my first line echoing in the dark auditorium, "What Fritz can do, I can do anytime." Even now, I recall the sound of my voice ringing out in the small theatre and the unexpected laugh that greeted it. That was a lovely and pleasant sensation, but the theatre had not seduced me yet.

Still, fate did not let go. About 1915, the famous Yiddish actor Jacob Ben-Ami was to direct three one-act plays in Yiddish for the Neighborhood Playhouse, which was beginning to be thought of as a serious American theatre. The actors in the play were members of the Progressive Dramatic Club; and because I had worked with them before and spoke Yiddish, I was asked to join them. I played the part of a young man in a play by the great Jewish writer and playwright J. L. Peretz. I am only now familiar with the basic idea of the plot because I reread it many years later. Again, I have no recollection of what happened on stage, nor do I remember anything about the rehearsals. Curiously, I did not even carry away any observations or anecdotes of Jacob Ben-Ami, whose work was later to play an important role in the development of my awareness of acting.

My third experience on the stage was a more lasting memory for me. Once again, I cannot recall the name of the play nor what it was about, only that it was a German play by Hermann Sudermann. By that time the Progressive Dramatic Club had achieved a certain renown and distinction. They gave special performances in a regular theatre once a year. On this particular occasion the production was to take place in the old Liptzin Theatre on the Bowery, named after a famous Yiddish actress.

I remember the rehearsals only in the sense that I remember that there were rehearsals. I played the young brother of a woman who had an affair with a man outside of her class. Once the affair was over, the man paid little or no attention to her. The rehearsals were intellectual and analytical in nature and only set the movements of the scene. We did not rehearse with props. There was no dress rehearsal. The first time we were on the stage with the lights and the scenery was when the actual performance took place. The one particular moment from that play that remains vivid in my memory is the scene that preceded the romantic meeting between the woman and her lover. Perhaps I would like to forget it.

It is sundown. The stage is empty and I was supposed to enter to light the lamp to set the mood for the romantic scene that was to follow. I can remember as clearly as if it were happening now: walking over to the table in the center of the stage, facing the audience, and picking up a match to light the lamp. I looked at it and suddenly before me was a lamp I had never seen before. It was one of those old-fashioned lamps with a chimney. I had no idea of how to light a lamp of that kind. There was an opening only at the top. I put my hand into the top of the chimney with the match and . . . well, you know what happened. The chimney acted as a vacuum; the fire flared and almost exploded in the chimney. Beyond that moment, I haven't the slightest recollection of what actually happened. I seemed to be hovering in midspace. I could feel no floor under me, but in front of me were thousands of eyes, large eyes, pulsing toward me — the kind of thing you see in surrealistic paintings or in your nightmares. They moved, they grew larger as they came toward me, and then they receded. I saw no faces, just those eyes. I remember nothing else. I don't know how I got off the stage. I cannot recall if there was a scene in the play after that involving me. Of course, I don't remember how the lamp finally was lighted.

Had I at that time any serious expectations of working in the theatre, the experience with the lamp probably would have demolished them. I was fortunate that my interests in performing on stage had not yet developed.

I also remember another acting experience that took

place in a school I attended which taught both Yiddish and Hebrew and subjects relating to Jewish culture. The school's principal was Joel Antin, who was also the ideological head of the Progressive Dramatic Club and a real force in the intellectual life of the Jewish community. He was a strange, peasantlike man with a body and face that seemed carved out of clay. He had studied at Columbia University with a specialty in dramatic literature. He lectured to us about the history of Jewish drama, stressing its folk roots, its earthiness, and its sense of realistic characterization. It was as if one of the granite Egyptian statues was talking with a haunting, unchanging intensity. The impression he made on us youngsters was a powerful one.

On each holiday he would speak to us about the history and significance of that particular festival. On certain holidays — especially Purim and Chanukah — the school would perform little historical plays. I had obviously demonstrated some acting skill, because I was picked to play the part of Mordecai in a Purim play. At the end of the play one of my teachers came over to compliment me on my performance. Then another teacher came over and started berating the other one for complimenting me. He told him that he shouldn't turn my head with fables of that kind. "It is nonsensical to give any young man the idea that he should be interested in the theatre. This is not a serious ambition to hold up to any young man as an ideal." I was perplexed and startled that anyone would take exception to my being complimented — or might think that I would have any serious interest in going into the theatre.

Yet, without my realizing it, I was to start to succumb to theatre's call. At the beginning of the twenties I was a young man. More than anything else, I was seeking some way of meeting certain people who shared my interests. Or put another way, I was looking for female companionship.

Some of my friends, knowing of my earlier theatrical experiences (they evidently were not aware of my traumatic lamp-lighting episode), told me that they were organizing a dramatic club at the Chrystie Street Settlement House. The settlement house at that time was an interesting phenomenon. It offered an opportunity for many youngsters to engage in athletic and cultural fields that were not available to them otherwise. This particular club was to be called "Students of Art and Drama," or, as we shortened it, without any awareness of acronyms of the future FDR days, the S.A.D. Of course, the club's primary function was more social than dramatic, but it did represent a desire on our part to be connected with cultural aspects of our community and to participate in some intellectual activities. As I have said, this was one of the strongest motivating factors in the life of the East Side.

Philip Loeb, who was at that time the casting director for the Theatre Guild, came to one of the performances at the settlement house to see an actor friend of his in a one-act play I also had a part in.

I played the role of a young blind boy. At the end of the performance when Loeb came backstage to see his friend, he looked at me, sort of examining me, then said quietly, "Are you interested in being in the theatre?" I answered very simply and sincerely, "No." He didn't shrug his shoulders or respond in any way. "Well, if you are, look me up." I promptly forgot that meeting until some years later when I did indeed look him up — but that, of course, is the beginning of another story.

I still did not in any way see myself as an active participant in the theatre. I had no special skill that I was aware of. I was working as a shipping clerk and doubling as a bookkeeper for a small business which sold human hair to large stores such as Woolworth's and Kresge's. While I didn't quite know what my future was going to be,

I looked forward to some type of intellectual activity—perhaps being a teacher of some kind.

I continued to attend the theatre. Occasionally I went to the Yiddish Theatre, but these performances left only faint impressions. I do remember clearly an actor of great temperament, David Kessler. I saw Jacob P. Adler toward the end of his life. He was a magnificent-looking . . . I was going to say human being, but you hardly thought of him as a human being; you thought of him as an actor—someone grand, unusual, leonine in appearance.

My real theatre-going memories started and continued with the Broadway theatre, and coincided with my decision to become an actor. The first Broadway play I saw was a Thanksgiving matinée performance of Walter Hampden in *Hamlet*. I went with one of my best friends, Ben Slutsky (our friendship went back to my early youth and lasted well into the Group Theatre days, when he passed on). We naturally asked for cheap tickets. Since the house was not full, we were given orchestra seats. Hampden's performance was impressive: it was traditional, yet not superficial. This, then, was my first *Hamlet*.

I was fortunate to begin my Broadway theatre-going at a time still considered a golden age of acting. I saw the work of Eleanora Duse, Giovanni Grasso, Laurette Taylor, and other great performers. I do not know how, but even at that time I possessed a good observation and awareness of acting. I could tell the difference between what was real and true, and what was only external skill. In view of the fact that I remember so little about the plays that I was involved in, it is odd that I remember so clearly certain performances I saw.

One of the great defects of the theatre is that what is created in it is written in melting snow, and that only memories remain of the experience. In those early days, I remember with great pleasure, and some degree of nostalgia, seeing the performance of Eva Le Gallienne in *Liliom.* I wish it were possible still to see the young Eva Le Gallienne, and that strange ethereal quality she possessed on the stage.

We tend to think of it as a modern phenomenon for an actor to portray characters who cannot express their feelings, yet these were precisely the parts that Miss Le Gallienne played in those days. She was perhaps less naturalistic than young actors are today. Yet, there was a quality of pure poetry created by her presence and behavior.

One of the great performances of that time and of my theatre-going experience was that of Jeanne Eagels in *Rain.* By a "great performance" I mean one which does not simply follow the shape and outline of the character and events, but in which the reality, experience, and intensity of the emotions of the character seem to be perfectly gauged by the actor. It not only seems to be, but actually is, being created by the actor at that particular moment and shared with us, the audience.

That performance has remained so clearly in my mind that many years later, when I became associated with the late Marilyn Monroe, *Rain* was the first production that we planned to do after her contract with Fox was finished. In fact, we had come close not only to planning but to arranging a production as a television special with Miss Monroe. Unfortunately, through no fault of our own, it never came to pass.

It is one of my deep sorrows that the public never was able to see her in that and other plays which we had the good fortune to see her in at the Actors Studio and in my private classes. It was my feeling that she would have come close to creating both the earthiness and sensuality and the strange striving that Jeanne Eagels had originally created in that part. When others tried to play it (for instance, Tallulah Bankhead), they tended to capture only the external characterization, the vulgarity of the part. No one seems to remember the inner, almost mystic flame which engulfed Eagels in the scene with the preacher. It seemed as if she had been brought up to some new dimension of being, so that when she found to her great shock and surprise that he was concerned with what she had left behind — the lusts of her body — her sense of loss and her disillusion were overwhelming.*

The actress Pauline Lord, who appeared both in Eugene O'Neill's *Anna Christie* and later in Sidney Howard's *They Knew What They Wanted,* gave what I remember as being complete, unified, effortless, and revealing performances. Yet in most of her later work there was a mechanical, dead quality. We would wait through a whole performance before there would be a moment — an electrifying one — when it seemed that a switch had been pulled. Emotion would flare. Then the acting would continue, easily, simply, naturally, but quite unmoving and unmoved. As Lord's career unfolded, she began to develop a hesitation waltz. She would stop and start through a performance. When I met her years later, I had the feeling she was a person waiting for something to happen. Her voice was husky, her eyes luminous, looking for something they never found. When her performance was complete, it was electric. When it wasn't, it was empty — seemingly natural, but formless and, in a way, lifeless.

I have no memory of Laurette Taylor's Broadway work, though I am sure I must have seen it. But years later, when

---

* I am sometimes very annoyed that when some young actress makes a first appearance on the stage, she is touted as a "young Jeanne Eagels." Either people making such a claim never saw Jeanne Eagels or they don't remember what they saw, because there was no such thing as a "young Jeanne Eagels." When she was young no one knew about her. Only when she became older did she become Jeanne Eagels as we think of her. And to throw that albatross around the neck of any young actress gives her an impossible burden to bear; I have seen many flounder under that kind of pressure.

I was in Chicago, I was told about her performance in *The Glass Menagerie*. Luther Adler had seen it there and made a point of telling me not to miss it. I had the unusual good fortune of seeing her in what turned out to be her last performance in that part. This *was* a great performance; but the greatness cannot be explained by anything that the actress did. Many people have tried to describe what her acting was like. They usually wind up saying, "Well, it wasn't anything that she did; it wasn't in fact any *one* thing. It just ... it just was." Curiously enough, this was an accurate description. What these people were trying in some way to express was a sense that Taylor's performance was an experience, that it was a person living, breathing on stage, not acting. Some of the actors in the play told me that at times they themselves didn't know exactly what Taylor would say next. If anything, it was the fact that it was not acting which made it great acting.

Only in the case of Eleanora Duse had I experienced something akin to Taylor's work, but Duse's acting had a different intention and awareness. The appearance of Eleanora Duse on Broadway was a great historical moment for me and many others. On the basis of previous experiences, I had somehow learned to recognize great acting. Now, I was prepared to see what amounted to the most extraordinary performer of her time.

Ibsen's *The Lady from the Sea* was Duse's first performance in New York in the early twenties. *The Lady from the Sea* played at the old, huge Metropolitan Opera House. I sat two-thirds of the way back in the orchestra, but Duse's voice floated easily through the theatre. It was somewhat high-pitched. Having had difficulty with her voice in her youth, she had trained herself to use it in some particular fashion. What was extraordinary was that the voice did not seem to be projected toward you; rather, it seemed simply to float toward the audience.

I waited throughout the evening for these moments — for the great temperamental eruptions, that intense emotional throb — that I had learned to recognize as a part of great acting. But there was none of that in *The Lady from the Sea*. What I did see was something unusual: a presence, a sense of something taking place before my eyes that was at once fleeting in its presentation but frozen in my awareness. It was like a lingering taste.

When I walked away from the performance, I had a somewhat confused reaction, a conflicting response. Certainly what I had seen was something unusual, but where was the acting that I had come to expect? Where were the characteristic moments of emotional outburst? At that time, I did not know the play well, and it was acted in Italian. But I remember thinking that at the moment when Duse pleaded with her husband to permit her to go away with the stranger, and he finally consented, the most wonderful smile shone on her face. Duse had a strange way of smiling. It seemed to come from the toes. It seemed to move through the body and arrive at the face and mouth and resembled the sun coming out of the clouds. When she smiled, I thought to myself: "This is really what the play is about. This is really what she wanted all the time. She didn't really want to go. She just wanted freedom to choose." And as I kept thinking over that scene, it suddenly occurred to me: "What am I saying? I saw a play that I don't really know, in a language that I don't really understand, and the actress told me what the play is all about." Duse demonstrated to me that acting was not only emotional outbursts or even the presentation of the depth of emotion. In her, I saw a moment-to-moment awareness of the life of the character. Duse had the most extraordinary facility of just sitting on the stage and creating a person who was thinking and feeling, without that particular intensity that ordinarily characterizes emotional behavior.

The next play I saw Duse in was Henrik Ibsen's *Ghosts*. I can still see her as Mrs. Alving sitting on the sofa talking to Pastor Manders. Her chin was supported on her hand in a thoughtful gesture which has been caught by some of the photographs of her. Here was a person sitting, thinking, talking; and without my being able to follow the text of the play, it was very clear that the words were sounding within her. Duse was able to find gestures which were not simply natural, but most expressive of what would be difficult to suggest any other way. In Act I, when Mrs. Alving looks off stage, she spies Oswald flirting with Regina; suddenly the hidden past appears before her. It was as if waves swept on the stage and enveloped Duse at that moment. Her arms suddenly brushed upward as if the wall was falling on her. But her hands flailed hopelessly, as if the wall were made of cobwebs that clung to her hands and enveloped them. She seemed to be struggling to free herself.

With her gestures, Duse was not only real, she was also revealing the theme of each play, or each scene. Of all the actors I have seen, Duse was the most perceptive in trying to embody the theme of the play.[*] Her gestures often became a heightened expressiveness. The near-great actor Michael Chekhov called these kinds of gestures "psycho-

[*] Many years after I had seen Duse, I was taken by Clifford Odets to meet Charles Chaplin. Chaplin seemed to me the epitome of the professional actor. He couldn't do anything just by talking. His discussions were always accompanied by demonstrations that he illustrated with his entire being. Clifford tried to involve me in their conversation.

"Lee, why don't you tell Charlie your memories of Duse." That was all that was necessary to set Chaplin off. In the next hour, Chaplin demonstrated all the styles of acting, the difference between Japanese and Chinese acting, the way in which Italian actors worked always with a prop. He wound up with an imitation of Duse. Yet, this great mimic could not capture her style, because there was nothing that she did outside the scene and the character. She had no mannerisms of her own and therefore it was impossible to imitate her. She was merely a vehicle for the idea of the play.

logical gestures." For me, finding a way of achieving a heightened expressiveness has remained one of the paths in the search for the future of the theatre.

In these early days I was also greatly influenced by the great singing actor Chaliapin. I first saw him at a Saturday matinée in 1923 at the Metropolitan Opera House in a production of Mussorgsky's *Boris Godunov*. My seat was in the topmost gallery in the opera house, at the extreme end, close to the stage. I could hardly see anything. I had to twist my head down and sideways to see what was happening on stage. Chaliapin was in particularly good voice, and it floated effortlessly up to the rafters and through my body. The opera *Boris Godunov* was not yet well known to audiences, so when Chaliapin's character recoiled from the unseen presence and tried to drive it from the stage by throwing a chair at it, some of the audience members rose from their seats to see who had unexpectedly entered the stage.

What was impressive to me was the fact that this performance was created within a strict external sequence and rhythm. I learned that this inner emotional experience that I had come to recognize as great acting could be created with behavior that was strictly bound by elements of rhythm or a musical framework. This discovery proved essential in my later work.

At the time, I had little knowledge of opera or of music generally. As a result, I concentrated on the acting styles. I was fortunate to attend the last stage performance of Frances Alda, and to hear Beniamino Gigli in *Faust*.

Somewhat later, I went with Clifford Odets to see Lotte Lehmann in Richard Strauss's *Der Rosenkavalier*. The flow of that performance revolved around Lehmann's delineation of the Marshall. Here was an inner characterization, one that I would have thought difficult to enact in opera; and yet Lotte Lehmann created psychological realities with all the elements expected from a stage performance. We enjoyed all of the performance enormously. They had a very good Baron Ochs and a Czech singer, Jarmila Novotna, whom Clifford took a liking to. Fritz Reiner's conducting produced a marvelously fluid and supple mood. When the waltzes were played in the third act, the whole opera house, including the chandeliers, seemed to dance with music. Clifford shared my excitement over *Der Rosenkavalier*. It was a cold night in December. After the performance we walked toward Lindy's Restaurant, a favorite of theatre people then. A shared lament was in our thoughts: Why couldn't the theatre be as exact as the opera is, where every detail is perfect?

One of the most exciting performances I remember was that of Jacob Ben-Ami in *Samson and Delilah*. It remains for me the greatest single modern performance that I have experienced, and I am not alone in that opinion. By "modern" I mean that Ben-Ami's performance caught the peculiar, divided, dual quality of modern man.

The play itself is not of a first-class calibre. It deals with the life of a young playwright who has written an allegorical drama called *Samson and Delilah*. The playwright's wife is the leading actress in the play; she is secretly in love with another man. At the rehearsal of the play, the playwright-director is dissatisfied with the actor playing the role of Samson and reads the part himself. He is thrilled by the passion with which his wife reads her lines until he realizes that she is playing over his head to her lover, the leading man. On the one hand, he is thrilled by her acting, and on the other he is driven insane by his jealousy. He plans to kill the guilty lovers, but he weakens at the thought of taking a human life. Instead, at the end of the play, he sends a bullet into his own head.

The play is simple in outline, but offers wonderful opportunities for the actor. Pauline Lord was making her first appearance on Broadway as the wife, and Edward G. Robinson acted the part of the leading man. Ben-Ami as the playwright was particularly skillful at creating the outbursts of emotion, and had an equal capacity to create deep, simple, but quiet inner experiences.

In a scene in the last act of *Samson and Delilah*, the poet returns from wandering through the forest, by now wild with his anxiety. Ben-Ami came on stage with an inner quiver running through his entire body, yet at the same time he seemed physically tired and hungry. He picked up some food from the table — a herring — and I remember the relish with which he devoured it. The ferocity of his hunger mirrored the intensity of his torment. This power and vividness generated on the stage by Jacob Ben-Ami in *Samson and Delilah* I was not to see again until I later saw the great Sicilian actor Giovanni Grasso.

Ben-Ami had been magnificent in the role of the jealous playwright, yet, when I saw him in Franz Werfel's *Spiegelmensch*, there was little of the intensity I knew he was capable of supplying. Ben-Ami played the part of a tormented intellectual — a character very close to the one he had played in *Samson and Delilah*. He should have been excellent in this play, yet his performance was somewhat tepid. I knew something was wrong. Here, without fully realizing it, I was beginning to be aware of a basic problem in acting which I was to observe many times again: the problem of inspiration. This was long before I myself became concerned with it or before I had any knowledge of how it could be solved.

A production which was much more decisive in crystallizing my thinking on the subject was Ben-Ami's performance in a Philip Barry play, *John the Baptist.* Both the play and the performances received poor notices. Because of my admiration for Ben-Ami, I wanted to see the play and went to an actors' matinée. The audience was filled with many actors, including Katharine Cornell, whose husband, Guthrie McClintic, had directed the play.

Unfortunately, I had to agree with the critics. Ben-Ami's acting was strangely lifeless. He seemed to be going through the paces without any of the inner excitement I had previously seen him create. But what startled me was that during intermission, out in the lobby, Miss Cornell was dissolved in tears, telling the people around her that he had been so wonderful at rehearsal. She bemoaned the fact that this performance did not measure up. I remember being annoyed by this malarkey: "He had been so wonderful in rehearsal." I have since heard it often from actors. Now I am used to it. But at that time I had very little patience or understanding for that kind of reaction. After all, I reasoned, I was a devoted admirer of Jacob Ben-Ami, and nobody could tell me on the basis of the performance I had just seen that he could ever be good in this particular play.

The play was closing at the end of the week. I happened to be in the neighborhood of the theatre to meet an actor friend of mine, and I had arrived early for the appointment. At the theatre where *John the Baptist* was playing, the audience was standing out front, and people were just starting to go in for the last act. Instead of waiting outside for my friend, I decided to go in and stand at the back of the theatre. I caught the last act of the play, in which John is released from prison.

Ben-Ami came through a gate onto the stage. He assumed the same stance that I had seen him take before, leaning against the wall; but this time there was something different — an indefinable, inner, feverish vibration; weary but excited. A character asks John why he will not recant. As he answered, Ben-Ami bent down as if he were listening to something, as he had in the earlier performance. It was a purely mechanical gesture.

Then he spoke his line: "God tells me." The first time I saw this scene I had thought sardonically, "Yeah, God tells him." This time when he was asked the question, he again leaned down to listen. He started to say, "God tells ..." and a shiver ran through my spine because this was something totally different. The gesture was the same externally, physically; yet there was an inner life. It was a kind of scenic communication that we in the theatre would call inspiration. It had been completely missing in the first performance I had seen and obviously in the performance the critics had seen. What I was now seeing was something ineffable. I was forced to conclude that Miss Cornell may have been right. Silently, then and since, I apologized.

This experience left me with the questions What happened? How was it possible? How can an actor's performance suddenly change? Why couldn't Ben-Ami summon that inspiration for the matinée when all the actors were there clamoring, waiting to sympathize with him? What was the problem?

I soon found that the problem I had seen in Ben-Ami's performance was not limited to him. I had heard of an actor playing on Grand Street called Giovanni Grasso. I thought at the time I had discovered a great actor presumably nobody knew about. (Of course, I later found out that Stark Young and many other critics had written about him.) I first saw Grasso in an extraordinary performance of *Othello*. Tigerlike in his movements as he watched for signs of betrayal in Desdemona, Grasso demonstrated an overwhelming emotional range. Later I was to discover that the physical business and outline of this performance were taken from a great nineteenth-century actor, Tommaso Salvini. But Grasso's performance was so filled with passion, emotional intensity, and power that it never seemed like an imitation of anybody else's behavior. Grasso created reality with such physical and emotional conviction that it almost transcended what I thought of as acting.

Grasso's performance in a scene from *La Morte Civile* struck me as especially moving. He played a character who has just escaped from prison. The prisoner arrives on the scene tired and hungry. A young girl brings him some food and a flagon of wine. Grasso's character breaks the bread and starts to stuff it into his mouth. As he looks at the girl (I know this is impossible to believe, but this is what I saw), he falls in love with her in that one instant: love at first sight. Now this was great acting that I recognized; Grasso had created the character's inner realization. But what I especially remember was that at that moment the bread stuck in his throat. Now, with all honesty, I haven't any way of knowing whether the bread literally got stuck or whether he created that impression by his acting. The same action appeared at the end of the play when Grasso's character decides to take his own life by poison. The poison was in a little sack around his neck. I remember him putting the little pills into his mouth. The residue of the pills seemed to remain on his tongue as he swallowed them. Then, desperately, he tried to dislodge the poison from his throat. I don't know to this day whether the effect was created physically by the pills or by his acting. But certainly in the rest of the scene, he could only have relied on his acting skills. His death throes were so real, so convincing — his face drained of blood, his entire body convulsed. Yet these effects were not just physical: there was an emotional life that seemed to impel them. I had to hold on to the sides of my chair in order not to call out for help. It seemed to me that there was a man dying in front of me. At the end of the play, the curtain stayed down somewhat longer than usual. When it came back up, the actors took their bows; in the middle stood Grasso, still pale, still slightly trembling. The physical conviction and emotional reality which he had summoned was extraordinary, terrifying, and very exciting.

A few nights later I invited some friends to see Grasso's performance with me. When I say "invited," that is hardly the word, because I didn't buy their tickets; I barely had enough money to buy my own. But, nonetheless, I invited them to share this extraordinary experience. I felt I had discovered Grasso, and, therefore, I felt responsible for him. A number of people came, many of whom were later to become members of the Group Theatre. I remember Morris Carnovsky and Stella Adler being part of the group. As the first two acts of the performance went on, I sank deeper into my chair, hoping that no one would pay attention to me; it seemed that the great actor was having an off night. Grasso obviously knew the performance wasn't going well. This evidently didn't bother him, except that he did sort of run his hand through his sparse hair, expressing a slight dissatisfaction and self-consciousness. Grasso's attitude seemed to say, "I am not responsible for inspiration: that comes from above, and if you, the spectator, come on an off night, it is something that I cannot help." As a professional actor, Grasso was quite prepared for this type of event, but for me it was a real calamity, a blow to both my ego and my reputation. There was no way in which I could demonstrate to my friends what it was that I had previously seen. As they kept turning to me during the first two acts, I sank even lower.

My embarrassment lasted until the end of the second act, or the beginning of the third, I do not remember which. At that point in the play, there is a confrontation between Grasso's character and his wife, who had fallen in love with his best friend. The play was in Italian and I was not watching it as much as I was watching the acting. The wife is seated on the bed. Grasso had an odd way at times of contacting the actress playing his wife. He would put his hand on her head and sort of lift her by the hair. I don't know whether that was Grasso-like or Sicilian. He walked over to her as he was talking to her, put his hand on her hair, and started to lift her. I have seen inspired performances, but I have not seen the moment of inspiration strike as suddenly as it did then. He touched her, and the touch seemed to create impulse. Suddenly, the blood rushed into Grasso's face; his eyes distended. This wasn't acting: this was real — real blood, real bursting of blood vessels. From that moment on, his face, his whole body, and his entire performance changed. I sat upright in my chair, willing to take bows. The great actor had suddenly proved that he *was* a great actor!

But for me the problem I had already encountered with Ben-Ami's performance remained: What was it that had happened? How was it possible for a man who had literally walked through the first acts of a part to suddenly come alive? Well, obviously he found his inspiration. But how had Grasso done this? Some actors are able to reach the highest level of creativity — call it inspiration if you wish. Yet there are times when this inspiration leaves them; times when it does not happen; times when they have no ability to make it happen.

My growing awareness of and interest in the problems that I have described led me to begin to search for some answers. My personal experiences as a spectator and an amateur actor coincided with the rapid development of the modern American theatre. The twenties saw the formation of several important theatrical organizations: the Provincetown Players, which produced the work of Eugene O'Neill; and the Theatre Guild, which helped elevate the American stage to the level of the best European theatre. I began, also, to read a great deal of new material which described the modern movements that were taking place. Through books written about theatre, a whole new world opened up for me.

The first book I read was Hiram Motherwell's *Theatre of Today*. Published in 1914, it was a short summary of what was taking place in the world theatre. Essentially, it focused on Europe, which was the foundation of our own early development. Already twentieth-century theatre was feeling the effects of two visionary stage designers and a director. These new names that already seemed legendary were included in Motherwell's history: Edward Gordon Craig, the apocalyptic Englishman who was to revolutionize scenic design in the twentieth century, wrote about scenic innovation and illustrated his concepts with his own imaginative sketches; Adolphe Appia, a mysterious figure who revolutionized the concept of stage lighting by calling light an additional actor on stage; and Max Reinhardt, who was equally at home directing a dance pantomime or a massive theatrical spectacle. Other books which I devoured with similar interest were the works of Huntly Carter — *The New Spirit in Drama and Art* and *The Theater of Max Reinhardt* — and books by Sheldon Cheney. Above all, there was the work of Kenneth MacGowan and Robert Edmond Jones, early founders of the Provincetown Players. In *Continental Stagecraft* they described what they had seen during one year's travel on the Continent. This opened my eyes to a whole new world.

Since I was never entirely satisfied with secondary material, these readings led me to the original sources.

The writings of the designer Edward Gordon Craig were the most influential in this regard. It would be no exaggeration to say that they became the strongest intellectual stimulus for me to devote my life to the theatre. There has been a great deal of confusion as to the significance of Craig's work. Craig's designs for the theatre sought to capture the emotional life of the play and to express that life in abstract forms. Most people still think of him as an impractical visionary who put into words what he could not accomplish on the stage. Despite the fact that he came from a theatrical family — he was the son of the famous English actress Ellen Terry — Craig was always on the periphery of the professional theatre. He made impossible and innovative demands while refusing to compromise his own ideas. It is fashionable to point to the designer Lee Simonson's criticism of Craig. Simonson analyzed Craig's sketches and tried to show that they were completely utopian and could never be carried out on stage. However, Craig himself always pointed out that these sketches were imaginary and theoretical.

Many people in the theatre were beginning to make greater aesthetic demands on the medium, but few knew how those demands could take a form on the stage. It was in this area that Craig's ideas were of enormous significance. It was Craig who in his drawings and manifestos showed that intentions and ideas could be embodied in actual shapes and forms. For him everything in the theatre — the lighting, the setting, the acting — became part of a larger unit that comprised the art of the theatre. For Craig, "scene design" was "stage design" — something in which, on which, and within which the actor would act. "Scene design" must not simply define the background of the play or give an idea of the period in which it takes place. Rather, it must fit the needs of the action of the play, and it must help to motivate and make logical the behavior of the characters.

Craig addressed himself to the issue of acting as well. His concept of the actor was greatly misunderstood then and remains so now. In 1907, he wrote an essay called "The Actor and the Übermarionette" (Super Marionette). In the essay, Craig demanded that the actor must have the same precision that the marionette possesses. This concept

28

was considered insulting and downgrading to the actor's art. Even in my first reading of that essay, I never had that impression. The Super Marionette was not intended to replace the actor. On the contrary, the notion of it was to remind the actor that he must possess the precision and skill that the marionette *is capable of*. In other words, acting should be an art. I have always thought that Craig was right. I had already experienced the control that a great performer was able to exercise over his art in the great opera performances I have mentioned. For me, this demand of Craig's for responsibility, skill, and excellence became an abiding influence in my own search.

I had always been interested in other arts, but Craig's essays drew my attention to the way in which one can learn from great painters — Giotto, Goya, and Carpaccio, all of whom have a relevance to theatre. Craig's work also made me aware of theatrical history as a living experience. Craig himself collected theatre items that most people call "memorabilia." But for the theatre, they have more significance because they are the fossils of history — the means by which one can reconstruct the theatre of the past.

By opening my eyes to the possibilities of what theatre could and should be, Craig's work planted the motivation for my ultimately becoming a theatre professional. I was a young amateur when I first read his books; after finishing them, I wanted to achieve something different in my life.

I was still obsessed with finding out as much as I could about the problem of the actor. Even today there is still no serious history of acting, so I had to search for and find my way through material largely on my own. I began to read biographies of actors. The old ones especially had interesting descriptions of performances but threw very little light on the process by which the actors had arrived at these performances.

The material that seemed most enlightening turned out

to be the comments of the great drama critics of the past. The descriptions by Leigh Hunt, William Hazlitt, Henry Morley, George Henry Lewes, and George Bernard Shaw excited my imagination. I could almost see the great actors: Edmund Kean, Mrs. Siddons, Salvini, and Rachel.

As I began to delve further into the acting of the nineteenth century, I discovered that there was a central debate in terms of acting: Does the actor actually experience the emotion he is portraying, or should he demonstrate the emotion without experiencing it? The central participants in this debate were Henry Irving (the first English actor to be knighted) and Coquelin, the great French actor. Irving believed in the value of experience, Coquelin in the value of demonstration. This debate led to a book by William Archer called *Masks or Faces?*, which was really a survey of what actors thought about the debate.

I was startled to discover that in the eighteenth century — on the eve of the French Revolution — this same debate was taking place in France between two great French actresses. Mlle. Dumesnil was the leading exponent of emotional experience; Le Clairon, Voltaire's favorite actress, took what might be called the antiexperience position. Le Clairon contended that while there were moments when Dumesnil was inspired, the rest of the performance might be flat. Le Clairon demanded that the actor must not be swayed by temperament, but must rely on an external craft that remains solid.

As I continued my research into the problems of the actor, I realized that the debate between these two basic styles of acting — one demanding truthfulness of experience and of expression, and the other emphasizing the rhetorical and external nature of acting — appeared as early as Shakespeare's time. We find the debate summarized in many of Shakespeare's speeches, especially in Hamlet's well-known speech to the players (III, ii):

Speak the speech, I pray you, as I pronounced it to you, trippingly on the tongue. But if you mouth it, *as many of our players do,* I had as lief the town crier spoke my lines. . . . O, it offends me to the soul to hear a robustious periwig-pated fellow tear a passion to tatters, to very rags, to split the ears of the groundlings, who for the most part are capable of nothing but inexplicable dumb shows and noise. I would have such a fellow whipp'd for o'erdoing Termagant. It outherods Herod. Pray you avoid it. . . . *O, there be players that I have seen play, and heard others praise, and that highly (not to speak it profanely),* that neither having th' accent of Christians, nor the gait of Christian, pagan, nor man, have so strutted and bellowed *that I have thought some of Nature's journeymen had made men, and not made them well, they imitated humanity so abominably.*

The fact to notice is that while Shakespeare expresses his own ideals of truthfulness of emotion and expression, he is aware (as I've indicated in the highlighted phrases) that there are other actors who, while they possess none of the attributes he deems desirable, are nonetheless successful and highly regarded by the public. Even more significant is the suggestion in another of Hamlet's speeches. Hamlet has encouraged the player to demonstrate an example of his craft. As the player begins the speech, he is carried away by the sense and emotion of the words. When Hamlet is left alone he comments (II, ii):

> *Is it not monstrous that this player here,*
> *But in a fiction, in a dream of passion,*
> *Could force his soul so to his own conceit*
> *That from her working all his visage wanned,*
> *Tears in his eyes, distraction in his aspect,*
> *A broken voice, and his whole function suiting*
> *With forms to his conceit? And all for nothing!*
> *For Hecuba!*

The actor's emotions have stirred Hamlet's as well. This speech is a perfect illustration of the power inspired acting has over both the actor and the audience.

Molière, as well, refers to the same debate in his play *Impromptu at Versailles*. He contrasts the more experience-oriented methods of acting of his own company with those of the differing but nonetheless successful opposition. Molière's obvious intention is often lost in productions today because contemporary French actors usually perform in a style more reminiscent of that adopted by his opponents and thus dull the thrust of his satire.

The appearance of David Garrick on the English stage in 1741 signified a new understanding of acting not only in England but throughout Europe. Garrick, the first great naturalistic actor, became a strong proponent of emotional acting. Luigi Riccoboni's treatise on emotional acting versus declamation, first published in 1728 in Italy, was translated into English in the 1740s because it reflected the intellectual underpinnings of Garrick's performance style.

A few years later, in 1747, a major book on acting appeared: *Le Comédian*, by French journalist Ramón St. Albine. The book deals with the necessary qualifications of great performers: understanding (judgment or discernment), sensibility (or a disposition to be affected by the passions), fire (power, spirit, or vivacity), and a distinguished figure (though merit should be valued above personal charms). The book had a rather unusual history. In 1750, it was used as the basis for another work called *The Actor* by John Hill, which was revised in 1755 to *The Actor, or a Treatise on the Art of Playing*, to which were added "Impartial Observations on the Performance, Manner, Perfections and Defects of Mr. Garrick." The reputation of Garrick hovered so large over the eighteenth century that the work was then translated into French in 1769 by Antonio Sticetti and entitled *Garrick ou les Acteurs Anglais,* seemingly without any awareness that it was based on a French original. Sticetti's book, in turn, was compared to a book on acting published in 1750 by Francesco Riccoboni, son of Luigi.

All of this debate in the eighteenth century on the nature of the actor's problem provided the stimulus for the major essay on acting, *The Paradox of Acting* by Denis Diderot.

Diderot describes a very simple paradox: for the actor to move the audience, he must himself remain unmoved. The essay, therefore, seems to conclude that external acting is to be preferred to emotional acting.

When I first came in contact with the essay, it made no particular impression on me. I accepted the brilliance of its idea, but even that seemed useless in the face of the obvious incorrectness of his conclusion. After all, I had myself seen the effect created by inspired emotional acting in the performances of Ben-Ami, Grasso, and others. What forced me to reexamine my negative reaction was Stanislavsky's attention to the essay in his 1924 autobiography, *My Life in Art*. What could Stanislavsky possibly perceive in an essay that seemed so contradictory to his own theory and practice? I began to restudy Diderot's essay.

Diderot, in fact, started with a very simple and observable phenomenon. If sensibility (emotion) was the prime requisite for the actor, why was it that individuals highly gifted with this capacity were often most unable to act? Why was it that less sensitive people often became good actors? Diderot argued that the actress Le Clairon, when she first appeared, acted like an automaton; later, she gave fine performances. Diderot asked, "Did she acquire more soul, more sensibility, more heart as she grew older? And if so, why was it that when she returned to the stage after a ten-year absence she played but moderately? Had she

33

lost her soul, her sensibility, her heart?" What she had lost, Diderot suggested, "was the memory of her methods." I realized that what must have attracted Stanislavsky to Diderot's essay was the demand for a method of creativity.

This need for a method of consistently arriving at creativity seemed to point to an answer that I myself had been looking for.

Oddly, in a number of early essays and commentaries, Diderot had spoken of the need for real inspiration. In a letter written some years before *The Paradox*, Diderot had said, "If on the stage you do not feel that you are alone, the case is hopeless. . . . The actor who has nothing but reason and calculation is frigid. The one who has nothing but excitement and emotionalism is silly. What makes the human being of supreme excellence is a kind of balance between calculation and warmth. Whether on the stage or in ordinary life, the man who displays more than he feels affects ridicule rather than sympathy."

Diderot's basic proposition in *The Paradox of Acting* began with the problem, If an actor experienced real feeling in a first performance, he would be worn out and cold as marble by the third. This was not a theoretical assumption; it is precisely the problem that has faced all actors since time immemorial. Diderot went on to illustrate his point by citing "the unequal acting of players who play from the heart. . . . The playing is alternately strong and feeble, fiery and cold, dull and sublime; tomorrow they will miss the point they have excelled in today." Diderot noted that Dumesnil often went through a performance not knowing what she was doing, or what she was saying; yet she might reach one sublime moment of passion.

Diderot rightly asked the question, Can the actor laugh or cry at will? If the answer is no, then the actor must seek a different approach — a more external or mechanical means of achieving that result. Only if one can answer yes to Diderot's question can one legitimately question the paradox. The emotion, however, must derive not simply from the spur of the moment, but through some more controlled procedure. Diderot's conclusion was that this procedure could only rely on external means. But Diderot was forced to come to that conclusion because a real acting method was not available at the time he was writing.

Diderot went further in his idea that the use of real emotions was not possible on the stage. He referred to incidents when actors, in the midst of experiencing seemingly real emotions on the stage, had stopped to deal with secondary objects that were not part of the action of the play. Diderot asked: How is this possible if the actor is truly involved?

William Archer responded to this a century later. He argued that these signs of interrupted concentration actually proved the opposite. It is usually assumed that when a person's faculties are completely emotionally absorbed, he must be oblivious to everything else. On the contrary, the more intense an experience, the more likely the individual is to attend "with mechanical punctiliousness to the minutest trifles of everyday existence." The intensity of emotional response does not rule out awareness of other things that are going on. In the midst of severe crisis, an individual's attention will often register the smallest details related and unrelated to that crisis.

The real problem for the actor, therefore, is how to create in each performance the same believable experiences and behavior, and yet include what Stanislavsky called "the illusion of the first time." Diderot was aware that the man whom nature stamps as actor cannot reach the topmost height until the fury of the passions is subdued, until the head is cool and the heart under control. This coincided exactly with François Joseph Talma's basic definition of acting, "a warm heart and a cool mind," an epigram widely accepted as a correct formula for the actor's talent. But the central problem remained: How do you stimulate the heart to be warm? Shakespeare had expressed the difficulty of this task in the challenge to the actor to "force his soul so to his own conceit." Wordsworth had described the same difficulty (this time applying it to the poet's task) in his proclamation of the true voice of feeling: "emotion recollected in tranquillity." The one area that seemed to evade the actor's ability to deal with it technically as he dealt with the voice, body, or mental memory was feeling, emotion. (Stanislavsky was the first one to deal with this issue directly.) The brilliance of Diderot's exposition of the actor's problem explains the high regard for the essay despite the obvious inadequacy of the solution. I am inclined to think that Diderot himself recognized this. That may be the reason why he never published it. (It was discovered in the Russian archives and published in 1832.) The way in which his argument peters out at the end seems to me to suggest Diderot's own lack of belief in the logical but inadequate paradox. The problem that Diderot faced was the same one everyone in the theatre had been aware of. I have described the experiences that developed my own growing awareness. But with all the reading that I had done and all the observations of great actors that I was fortunate to make, plus my reading of pyschology, especially Freud and the Behaviorists, I was not aware of any solution.

The decisive step in my search for a solution to the actor's problem was the appearance of the Moscow Art Theatre in 1923–24. At the time the Moscow Art Theatre arrived in New York, the American theatre was at a high point. The physical productions of the Moscow Art Theatre were in no way equal to what we, at that time, saw on our own stage in the work of the great scene designers

Robert Edmond Jones, Norman Bel Geddes, Lee Simonson, and many others. The stage settings and costumes of the Moscow Art Theatre were literally tattered. In addition, the sets were poorly lit, and the makeup was exaggerated and much too noticeable under our modern lighting systems. Many audience members complained about these inadequacies.

Stanislavsky himself, in the letters that he wrote at that time, commented on the elaborate stage techniques and the extraordinary lighting which they had no knowledge of in Russia. Stanislavsky claimed that the extravagant productions of David Belasco would arouse envy from the Maly Theatre, the leading traditional theatre in Russia. He also marveled at the presence of actors like David Warfield, John Barrymore, and Laurette Taylor. He wrote that he had seen no one in Russia to compare with the young Joseph Schildkraut in *Peer Gynt*. Stanislavsky, therefore, was surprised by the extraordinary success the Moscow Art Theatre had in New York. He speculated that what had impressed New York audiences was the Moscow Art Theatre's approach to acting. Whereas the typical American production was built around a single star, the Moscow Art Theatre possessed three, four, and often more outstanding actors in the same production.

However, what had impressed me was something different. What completely bowled me over was not the acting of any of the great actors of the Moscow Art Theatre — I had already observed acting of greater dimensions, in the case of Chaliapin, Ben-Ami, Duse — but the simple fact that the acting on the stage was of equal reality and believability regardless of the stature of the actor or the size of the part that he played. Maria Ouspenskaya in *The Cherry Orchard* and Leo Bulgakov in *The Lower Depths* were true, real, and emotionally full, even in small roles. No matter what the nature and excellence of the ensemble created by other theatres and other productions, this equality of truth and reality created by each individual on the stage was, and remains, the unique contribution of the Moscow Art Theatre.

Obviously, this truth and reality was achieved by some singular process or procedure of which we in the American theatre had little knowledge. It seemed clear to me that what we were seeing was not just great acting, but something that embodied an approach to acting that might supply the answer to the problems that I had become aware of.

Let me share some details of my impressions of the Moscow Art Theatre. The first play I saw was the one with which the company had started its career, *Tsar Fyodor Ivanovitch.* I remember Stanislavsky's magnificent entrance in the role of Prince Ivan Shuisky: he wore chain mail and carried a great double-bladed sword. I was not too impressed with the physical production as a whole. The details of the costumes and stage design seemed archeologically correct rather than theatrically significant. With Craig's ideas of modern design in my mind, I was looking for something quite different in the contribution of the visual elements to a production. When I left the theatre, I carried away the image of Stanislavsky standing stage center, which has remained with me.

It was in the next plays that I began to see the genius of the acting of the company. They had brought to New York their greatest achievements, among them all the plays of Chekhov, with the exception of *The Seagull* (which for reasons I have not been able to discover had not been maintained in the repertoire).

The plays of Chekhov as performed by the Moscow Art Theatre were among the most complete embodiments of theatrical expression. This does not mean that I think they were perfect, or that I agree with the way in which they were interpreted; but I doubt that the minute, detailed, moment-to-moment aliveness on the stage represented by and participated in by every member of the cast will ever be achieved again — not because we do not have the talents, but because we do not have the means and the conditions. The plays had been done for many years and seemed as fresh as if they were being done for the first time.

In the productions that we saw in America, the plays were alive with vivid, intense, colorful experiences, while each moment was filled with marvelous creations of the experiences of the characters. There was never anything maudlin or pathetic or sentimental — nothing to suggest that Stanislavsky had deformed the Chekhov plays by turning them into tragedies.* I still see Stanislavsky as the doctor in *Uncle Vanya* standing in the center of the stage, his eyes slightly misty with drink, music in the background: Stanislavsky suggested an entire dance without ever moving his feet. In *The Cherry Orchard,* Leonidov as Lopakhin entered sturdy, plebeian, slightly drunk to announce with a mixture of defiance, apology, and triumph that he was the new owner. When Olga Knipper (Chekhov's wife) as Madame Ranevskaya waited for and received the news of the sale, she remained utterly still, without any suggestion of pathos or tragedy, but capturing the inner rhythm of the loss with no effort. The first act of *The Three Sisters* was a swirl of gaiety, charm, and hope.

The production of Gorki's *The Lower Depths* was amazingly theatrical. These characters were not aware of the

---

* I can only assume that those who have concocted this opposition between Chekhov and Stanislavsky based on the argument that Stanislavsky had drained the humor from Chekhov's work never saw the actual productions of the Moscow Art Theatre of that day. Or perhaps they are misled by Chekhov's comments based on his sensitivity, concern, and worry about the audiences' reception of his plays.

tragedy they were involved in. I remember Alyoshka's entrance as he danced into the room delightfully in his rose-colored togs — it was almost a vaudeville number. Katchalov as the Baron made every effort to retain his gentility . . . though his beard was spotted and untrimmed, his voice was cultured and caressing, and he wore a semblance of the remains of gloves on his hands. Stanislavsky as Satine reclined on a table center stage delivering propaganda speeches with flair and conviction, not just with ordinary sincerity.

Perhaps a point should be made about the acting of Stanislavsky. Some critics have evolved ingenious theories that his search for an acting method derived from his own supposed lack of talent. He is often compared to Katchalov, who always seemed to possess a natural romantic actor's quality on stage. I was fortunate to see Stanislavsky and Katchalov play the same parts: Gayev, the brother in *The Cherry Orchard*, and Colonel Vershinin in *The Three Sisters*. In both plays, Katchalov seemed more the actor than the character. Stanislavsky always seemed to fade into the character. Whether this was really a difference in acting approach or simply the fact that Katchalov always remained a star on the stage without making any special effort to accomplish it, I do not know.

In the Moscow Art Theatre, we saw for the first time the possibility of that greatness being shared by talents that were not necessarily on the same level, yet were capable of the same intensity, reality, belief, and truth. These experiences were a major factor in the stimulus toward further advances in the American theatre and were directly responsible not only for my own development, but for the creation of the Group Theatre, the Eva Le Gallienne Civic Repertory Theatre, the continuing efforts on the part of the Theatre Guild to create a repertory company without any real understanding of what a repertory company involved, and many other manifestations in the American theatre.

In 1924, as a result to a large extent of the visit of the Moscow Art Theatre, I finally decided to become a professional actor. I was ignorant enough to join a conventional theatre school, the Clare Tree Major School of the Theatre, where I practiced speech, voice, ballet, and other generally recognized requisites of the actor's basic training. At the end of the period I felt the need for something beyond that, but had no knowledge of where to find it. Another student in the school whose name I have unfortunately forgotten told me that he had come across another school in which he thought I would be interested. It seemed that two of the actors from the Moscow Art Theatre, Richard Boleslavsky and Maria Ouspenskaya, had decided to stay in America and organize a school called the Laboratory Theatre. Their aim was presumably to create a theatre in America based on the acting techniques practiced at the Moscow Art Theatre.

Before discussing the Laboratory Theatre, it is important, first, to understand the work of Constantin Stanislavsky, and to see how his approach to the problem of the actor had developed.

STANISLAVSKY AND THE SEARCH FOR HIS SYSTEM

THE teachings of Constantin Stanislavsky and his disciples changed not only my life, but that of the entire twentieth-century theatre. Just as our understanding of human behavior and modern physics is still turning on the revelations of Freud and Einstein, so our contemporary knowledge of the actor's craft is still heavily indebted to Stanislavsky's one-hundred-year-old discoveries. Probably no other name — besides Shakespeare's — is heard so often in the theatre. Yet Stanislavsky and his writings remain at the heart of a wild and frequently erroneous discussion of the actor's problems and training. Like the Bible, Stanislavsky's basic texts on acting can be quoted to any purpose.

Unlike Diderot, Stanislavsky cannot be thought of as a pure theoretician of the theatre. All of his work, all of his ideas, came from an empirical and practical understanding of the theatre. The problems Stanislavsky saw in the creation of a performance were derived from his own problems and those of his actors.

To understand Stanislavsky, to appreciate his clear-sighted and often ingenious answers to the central dilemma of the actor's art, one must first look carefully at Stanislavsky's own personal and professional development.

Even in his earliest acting experiences, Stanislavsky was aware of the problems of inspiration I had already observed in the performances of many great actors. He described an early experience in great detail in his autobiography, *My Life in Art*. At the age of fourteen, he performed in a small theatre his father had built on the family's country estate in Lyubimovka. He recalled his sensations while waiting for the play to begin. When he finally got on the stage, his heart thumped. Something inside of him drove him on, inspired him, and he rushed through the whole play. Words and gestures flew out of him with amazing rapidity. His breath failed him, he could hardly utter the words of his part, and he mistook his "nervousness and lack of restraint . . . for true inspiration." He was convinced that the audience was entirely in his power. At the end of the play he was surprised to find that the other actors avoided him. His performance had been a failure, although he himself had felt a real satisfaction in what he was doing on the stage.

Stanislavsky's awareness of what he had experienced was remarkably perceptive. He noted that the actor's state of mind is not always a true indication of what he is doing, nor of the impression he is creating on an audience. This self-awareness and the ability to determine the truthfulness of expression are fundamental demands of the actor's art and craft, since they must function at the very moment when he is actually creating. The moment of the creation must go hand in hand with the moment of evaluation. This is one of the most difficult problems for the actor to solve. Yet at this very early stage in his creative life, Stanislavsky was beginning to come to grips with this fundamental aspect of the actor's problem. This was a great first discovery. I emphasize Stanislavsky's use of the term *discovery* because too many ideas about acting are based on abstractions, on theories. Stanislavsky's ideas came from an analysis of his experience. Theory and practice were inseparable.

David Magarshack, who has written what is probably the best biography of Stanislavsky, doubts Stanislavsky could have learned all this from his very first performance in the Lyubimovka theatre. He suggests that Stanislavsky was probably summarizing impressions gained during the whole first period of his acting with what is known as the Alexeyev Circle of amateur actors. But it seems clear, from the notes that Stanislavsky made, that something happened on that definite occasion. Stanislavsky's description in *My Life in Art* may be clearer based on later knowledge and awareness, but the experience of that night was basic to the continuity of his search.

As Stanislavsky continued his amateur acting and directing, he constantly observed his own process of creation. He began to require his actors to live "in character" off stage. Yet the results were never fully satisfactory. Stanislavsky explained this problem: "The method of living a part in life demands continual impromptu, while the technical problem of learning a part by heart makes impromptu acting impossible." This, of course, is the centerpiece of Diderot's paradox. Stanislavsky empirically knew that the mechanical task of remembering the dialogue took up his emotional energy in performance. His attention turned to remembering his dialogue the moment he would hear his cues. As a result, the emotion could not keep pace with the words. Stanislavsky's awareness of this struggle constituted his second major discovery about the actor's problem, yet he was never able to resolve this fully.

By the age of twenty-five, Stanislavsky had established

the Society of Art and Literature, where he produced and acted in a number of plays. The major project he undertook in the 1895–96 season was *Othello*. As a director, Stanislavsky followed the same meticulous and elaborate preparations he had in other productions. He even journeyed to Venice in order to derive inspiration for the set design.

Throughout the rehearsal period, Stanislavsky was mentally tortured and physically exhausted. His own performance as Othello was a failure. (David Magarshack believes that Stanislavsky was simply incapable of the great tragic roles, that he lacked the necessary physical and emotional requisites for these characters. Having seen Stanislavsky in his great performances in the years 1923–24, and hopefully possessing some ability to perceive the possibilities of an actor's talent, I am unable to agree with that judgment.)

Stanislavsky himself suggested that his failure as Othello was really a failure to find the truth in his character. In *My Life in Art,* he noted that the great Italian actor Ernesto Rossi had come to see one of his performances as Othello. The next day Stanislavsky was invited to visit him. Rossi believed that Stanislavsky's elaborate re-creation of Venice had created a distraction. "It is necessary for those without talent," he told Stanislavsky, "but you do not need it." Stanislavsky described how the conversation continued:

> "God gave you everything for the stage, for Othello, for the whole repertoire of Shakespeare. . . . The matter is in your hands. All you need is art.". . .
>
> "But where and how and from whom am I to learn that art?" I questioned.
>
> "M-ma! If there is no great master near you whom you can trust, I can recommend you only one great teacher," answered the great artist.
>
> "Who is he?" I demanded.

"You yourself," he ended with the gesture he had made familiar in the role of Kean.

This advice was to leave a strong impression on Stanislavsky.

In 1897, Stanislavsky and Vladimir Nemirovitch-Dantchenko formed the Moscow Art Theatre. Their intention was to form a new kind of theatre unburdened by stereotypes and theatrical conventions.

In the early years of the Moscow Art Theatre, Stanislavsky seemed more concerned with detailed productions rather than in investigating the problems of the actor. Yet even in the company's first production, *The Seagull*, Stanislavsky sought out the logic and behavior of each character, and his sensory relationship to the objects that surrounded him. The production was heralded as a resounding success; Stanislavsky had located the logic of experience and of inner feeling which moderates external behavior, and from which true drama stems.

But Stanislavsky himself was not entirely satisfied. He had difficulty in finding the proper style and manner for the production of the plays of Maxim Gorki, especially *The Lower Depths* (1902), which was later to become one of the highest achievements of the Moscow Art Theatre. Stanislavsky was dissatisfied with his own performance in the role of Satine. He began to feel that often he was attempting to create original effects for the audience rather than properly interpreting the author's intention — that he was indulging in the New for the sake of the New.

Stanislavsky became impressed with the ideas of a young actor in the company, Vsevolod Meyerhold, who had by that time left the theatre and become a director. Meyerhold believed that he had found new ways and methods which, however, he could not realize because he needed strong actors. Stanislavsky organized a studio for him.

Although the studio ultimately failed, the attempt at systematic actor training was an acknowledgment that the theatre is first of all intended for the actor and cannot exist without him. For Stanislavsky it was the realization that "new actors were necessary, actors of a new sort with an altogether new technique."

For Stanislavsky the actor, his former joy in creation had waned. Somehow, the more he repeated his roles, the more he sank into a state of fossilization. It was in this frame of mind that he spent the summer of 1906 in Finland. He would spend his mornings on a cliff that overlooked the sea and take stock of all his artistic past. It was here that he made another discovery. He realized that the emotional content that was part of a role when he first created it was very different from the emotional content that he brought to the role with the passage of time.

Of special importance for him was the role of Dr. Stockmann in Ibsen's *An Enemy of the People*, which he had played with great success in 1900. The role had originally come easily for him. He had been particularly influenced by its political and social implications. He has also been stimulated by an altogether different line of action in the play: the love of Stockmann for truth. He sincerely sympathized with Stockmann as the character became more and more lonely with each succeeding scene. When, at the end of the performance, Stanislavsky as Stockmann at last stands alone, the line "He is strongest who stands alone" seemed to rise spontaneously from some inner power rather than any actor's intention. Stanislavsky felt himself more at home on the stage in the role of Stockmann than in any other role in his repertoire. In it he had followed his intuitions. To him Stockmann was not a politician, not an orator at meetings, not a reasoner, but a man of ideals, a true friend of his country and of his people. From this intuition had come the outer image of the character.

When Stanislavsky had first started to prepare the role of Stockmann, he had only to think of the cares and thoughts of the character and certain physical elements came of themselves — the forward stoop of the body, the near-sightedness that spoke so eloquently of his inner blindness to human faults. He automatically felt the childlike and youthful manner of movement, the quick step; the index and middle fingers of the hand stretched forward of themselves as if to push his own thoughts, feelings, and words into the soul of his listener.

All these characteristics had come to Stanislavsky unconsciously and without any effort on his part. But sitting on the bench in Finland, he accidentally struck on the feeling of the Stockmann long lost in his own soul. He realized that the perception that he had put into the role of Stockmann had been taken from living memories. He had drawn on his memory of one of his friends, an honest man whose inner conscience would not permit him to do what was demanded of him by the great of this world. "On the stage during the playing of the role these living memories used to guide me and always and invariably awoke me to creative work." He realized that as he continued to play the character, he had forgotten these living memories and that he remembered only the externals of his characterization. He had mechanically repeated these fixed appurtenances of the role and the physical signs of an emotion that had become absent. In some scenes, he had tried to act nervous and somewhat exalted, and for this purpose he had made quick, nervous movements. In others he had tried to look naïve and to do so had mechanically imitated childlike and innocent eyes. He had copied naïveté, but he was not naïve. He moved his feet quickly, but did not experience any inner hurry that might have caused short, quick steps.

This led Stanislavsky to examine how he had proceeded

in the early stages of creating a role. He reread the notes in his artistic diary, which reminded him of the experiences he had had. He remembered that the makeup and the physical image for the role of General Krutitsky in Ostrovsky's *Enough Stupidity in Every Wise Man* had been inspired by the general appearance of an old house he had once seen. It stood somewhat askew in an older courtyard and it seemed swollen with age; the overgrowth of moss at the corners looked like side-whiskers. From the house, little old men dressed in uniforms and carrying unnecessary papers under their arms would rush in and out. All of this had brought him in some mysterious way to his makeup for the comic role of Krutitsky. The material for the outer image was taken unconsciously from memories, as it had been in the role of Stockmann. But when he compared these notes of the initial creation to what remained in his soul while he acted the role, he was amazed how his performances were disfigured by bad theatrical habits and tricks, by the desire to please the public, and by incorrect methods. It became clear to him that for the actor not only physical makeup but spiritual makeup was necessary before every performance.

It was in this mood that the forty-three-year-old Stanislavsky returned to Moscow and embarked on the solution to the problem that was to become his obsession. He started to watch himself closely. He watched other actors when he rehearsed his new parts or their new parts with them. He had become aware that creativity on the stage demanded first of all a special condition, which he called "the creative mood." Of course, he and other actors before him had always recognized this intellectually, but he now realized this through his own experience and therefore, as he himself put it, "first perceived a truth long known to me." However, this creative mood did not seem to be subject to the control of the actor's will. It was considered

49

inspiration, a gift of the gods. Nevertheless, Stanislavsky asked himself, "Are there no technical means for the creation of the creative mood so that inspiration may appear oftener than is its wont?"*

What Stanislavsky sought was to find those conditions under which inspiration was most likely to enter into the actor's soul, and to learn how to recreate those conditions for each performance. It was necessary that inspiration be summoned by means of the actor's will.

As a first step for creating conditions under which inspiration could occur, Stanislavsky began to develop relaxation techniques in his own acting work. He compared his feelings in this new, relaxed state to those of a prisoner whose chains, which had interfered with his movements for years, had at last been removed. He sincerely believed that in relaxation "lay the whole secret, the whole soul of creativeness on the stage. . . . All the rest would come from this state and perception of physical freedom."

Stanislavsky was somewhat disconcerted that neither his fellow actors nor the audience noticed the change which he believed was taking place in his acting. Nonetheless, he continued his research and his own exercises until the habit of a free physical creative mood on the stage grew stronger and became second nature. Stanislavsky began to understand the function relaxation played in performance. He realized that he felt comfortable on the stage because, by centering his attention on the perceptions and situations of his body, he was drawing his attention away from what was happening on the other side of the footlights — beyond the black and terrible hole of the proscenium arch. He ceased to be afraid of the audience.

---

* That statement should not be interpreted to imply that he sought to create inspiration by exterior means; that would be impossible.

At times he almost forgot that he was on stage. He noticed that at such times, his creative mood was the most pleasant.

A second discovery soon followed. As Stanislavsky was watching the performance of a visiting star in Moscow, he felt the presence of the creative mood in the star's performance: there was a freedom of his muscles in conjunction with a great general concentration. The actor's entire attention was on the stage alone. Stanislavsky and the rest of the audience were attentive to every detail on stage. Stanislavsky realized that the more the actor's attention is on the audience, the more the audience will sit back in comfort awaiting attention. However, as Stanislavsky discovered with this performance, the concentration of the actor draws out the concentration of the audience, and, in turn, forces the actor to become concerned with what is happening on the stage. It excites his attention, his imagination, his thinking processes, and his emotion. He noticed that the concentration of the actor enhanced not only his sight and hearing, but all the rest of his senses — touch, taste, smell, the motor senses. That evening revealed the greater value of concentration for the actor. Accordingly, Stanislavsky began systematically to develop his concentration with the help of exercises he defined for that purpose.

As Stanislavsky continued to examine the creative mood of the actor, he noted the dilemma of trying to create a truthful emotion while being surrounded on the stage by imitation — scenery, cardboard, paint, makeup, properties, wooden goblets, swords and spears. Part of the actor's dilemma, therefore, is how to create truth from imaginary objects. The actor is concerned with the truth of his relation to the event on stage, to the properties, to the scenery, to the other actors who are appearing with him, and to their thought and emotions. Stanislavsky developed a mechanism to help the actor accept the truthfulness of the elements — the "creative if." According to Stanislavsky, the actor knows that the elements on stage are false, but he tells himself, "*If* they were true, I would do this and this, I would behave in this manner and in this way toward this and this event. . . ." I do not believe that this mechanism of the "creative if" always works; in fact, it often leads the actor to an imitation of what he thinks he would do. But what I believe is important is Stanislavsky's recognition of the dual nature of the actor's experience.

Many people have assumed that Stanislavsky's emphasis on the actor's need to experience truly is predicated on the assumption that the actor is not aware of the imaginary nature of the performance. In other words, the actor forgets that he is acting. Obviously, this is impossible. If the actor really forgot that he was acting, he would naturally drop his cues, his dialogue, and all of the scenic directions. What mattered, Stanislavsky felt, was the truth of the actor; it is what the actor feels and experiences internally that expresses itself in what the character says and how he reacts externally.

As a result of this discovery, Stanislavsky began consciously to apply all of his attention to the inner feelings of the character. As a director, he sought the unseen, unembodied passion that was born naturally in the soul of the actor. He eliminated staging and blocking from rehearsals in an effort to have the actor live with the strength of his own temperament and his own passion.

It was at this time that Stanislavsky started to put in writing the first elements of his "grammar of the dramatic art" that was to become known as "the system." In a letter to Nemirovitch-Dantchenko of November 16, 1910, he mentioned the previous professional envy, vanity, and intolerance which he hoped would give way at a riper age to experience and wisdom. He went on to share with Dantchenko some of his ideas about his system, maintaining that before it could be dissected, it had to be assessed in general from the literary, psychological, social, and living point of view.

Only after that is done can one divide it first into physiological units and then on the strength of that into psychological units or wishes. I know a few practical methods now (because it is my purpose of finding a way to realize every theory. Theory without realization is not my field and I abandon it), to help the actor in his psychological, physiological, living, and even social analysis and appreciation of the play and the role. But the literary analysis is up to you. You must make it not only as a writer and critic but as a practical man. We want a theory backed by a practical and thoroughly tested method.

All I know so far is before tackling my system we must: a) induce the volitional process; b) induce the process of searching — in a literary conversation (which is up to you), for I know how to sustain and develop the process of searching; c) I know how to induce the emotional process; d) I do not yet exactly know how to help the process of embodiment, but I have explored the ground and seem to be on the point of finding the way; e) the processes of synthesis and influence are clear.

It is up to me now to find a practical way of exciting the actor's imagination in all these processes. This aspect is very poorly developed in. psychology — especially the creative imagination of actors and artists. As for the rest, I think all of it is not only developed, but also quite thoroughly checked. I believe you will agree with me in all respects. Much of what you are told by third parties had reached their reason — but perhaps not their senses. In that lies the main difficulty. It is not hard to understand and remember. It is hard to feel and to believe.

The actual work on his system was enormously aided by Leopold Sulerzhitsky, who became Stanislavsky's assistant. Stanislavsky chose Sulerzhitsky to begin teaching his system in one of the private dramatic schools in Moscow. The experiment was so successful that several of Sulerzhitsky's students joined the Moscow Art Theatre and became the nucleus of the Second Studio.

Soon after the formation of the studio, Nemirovitch-Dantchenko announced to the entire company of the Moscow Art Theatre that all of Stanislavsky's new system of work should be studied by the actors and accepted by the theatre. The actors rebelled against this suggestion. Stanislavsky himself was forced to agree that they were right. He was not quite prepared for this program. In having changed his habitual manner of work in order to experiment, Stanislavsky's own acting had become less effective, and even the audiences had become aware of this. Stanislavsky realized that he had not yet found the right tools to build a road — not to the mind, but to the heart of the actor. Nonetheless, he continued to experiment.

A few years later, a studio production of Dickens's *The Cricket on the Hearth* included many young actors who had been exposed to Stanislavsky's experiments, among them Michael Chekhov and Eugene Vakhtangov. For the first time Stanislavsky heard those deep and heartfelt notes of super-conscious feeling that he had been striving for. The old actors of the Moscow Art Theatre began to pay a great deal more attention to Stanislavsky's pronouncements about the new methods of acting. His ideas began to ripen and become more precisely phrased and defined.

In 1920, after the revolution, when the world of the

theatre was nationalized, Stanislavsky was invited to present and demonstrate his ideas to the actors and singers at the Moscow Opera Theatre as a series of lectures. It is from this time that we possess the first coherent presentation of Stanislavsky's system. Notes from these lectures taken by one of the participants contain the first precise examples and descriptions of Stanislavsky's actual procedures in a simple and clear form. In these lectures, Stanislavsky outlined the processes of concentration, relaxation, and emotional memory.

In describing the most elementary point about the nature of the creative work of the actor, Stanislavsky emphasized the basic need for concentration on the stage. He emphasized that it is impossible to concentrate without first having practiced the exercises with imaginary objects. Imaginary objects are precisely that — objects which human beings deal with literally in life, and which the actor has to learn to recreate without the presence of the actual object. Before the actor starts work on the actual play with visual or living objects, he must devote some time to exercises on "concentrated attention with imaginary objects"; the actor must note every physical action and every sensation associated with that object. Stanislavsky stressed that for the actor "to know" means only to be able "to do"; and that one is able to do a thing only if one can control one's will, imagination, attention, and energy. Stanislavsky implied that this is not only part of the actor's training, but of the actor's actual work on a role.

Stanislavsky gave the following description of how concentration is to work:

According to the plot of the play, you have to kill your rival. Your thought, divided between the weapon and the action, will not permit you to forge that unity of action out of your body and energy which should have for the audience the stamp of truth; i.e., just thinking about the thought and what you want and so on will not accomplish the things that an actor always desires to accomplish. The only thought — the first one — which should enter your circle of concentration is your knife. Concentrate on the physical action; i.e., this is when you are already working on a scene with an actual prop, examining the knife; look at it closely, test its edge with your finger, find out whether its handle is firm or not. Transfer it mentally into the heart or chest of your rival; if you play the villain, try to estimate the force of the blow which will be needed to thrust the knife into your rival's back. Try to think whether you will be able to deal the blow, whether the blade should not have been a little bit stronger or whether it would stand the blow without bending. All your thoughts are concentrated on one subject only: the knife, the weapon.

When you have gathered all your power of thought on the knife, you can begin to widen the circle of your concentrated thought. Do not attempt to change anything in your state of mind, but transfer the thought from your knife to its object; in this case, to your rival. Here your thought will stumble by itself upon the memory of your first suspicion, when he who is now your enemy was still your friend.

Do not change the circle. Widen it. Let your thoughts sink deep into your memories. Do not however look for sombre colors just because you are acting the murderer and you want to kill your enemy. Allow your memory, your thought, to paint you the picture of your former friendship with your rival, transform yourself in your imagination to the days of your childhood when your friendship with him began, picture to yourself the loving faces of your mother and of his mother, and so on and so forth. You have concentrated hard on your memories, you forgot all about your knife, it is still in your hand, suddenly you cut your hand with it and all those beautiful thoughts fortified by the bright picture of your past are shattered. Your attention is once more reverted to the knife. And a whole gamut of new feelings which are now aroused by the memories of your rival's betrayal, deceit, and lies start tormenting you.

Stanislavsky suggested that it is only by this procedure that the actor will overcome the most vulgar preoccupation of all: stage fright. If the actor is fully concentrated on his objects, physical and otherwise, and is completely absorbed in the various problems set for him by his part or his director, he will simply not have the time to worry whether he will be able to act his part or what the audience will think of him or how awful it feels to walk on the stage where everyone can see and criticize.

Stanislavsky repeated another of the first principles of what was to become his system: relaxation. The one quality all the great actors had that he had been privileged to see and observe was their extraordinary freedom of movements, their ability to control their bodies with astonishing simplicity and flexibility. They seemed almost not to be playing before an audience, but to be living in their own environment without noticing anything that was unrelated to their immediate physical action or to the people with whom they were acting the play. Stanislavsky described this relaxation in the following way:

Movements on the stage that are absolutely free and unimpaired — i.e., movements without tension — that is the first thing a student-actor has to master. Having concentrated your thoughts on a definite problem and your attention on a definite group of muscles, you have to acquire the ability to move about in such a way that it should seem as though all your energy had been concentrated on those muscles.

Many people who suffer from physical, mental, or emotional tension are not aware of the degree to which they can learn to deal with and to control such tensions. Stanislavsky described this point in great detail:

Let us assume that you have to cross over from your place by the window and hide a letter you have just received but not had time to read through properly, so that those who are listening to your every move in the next room should not notice it. What are your problems? First of all, you have to get up without making any noise. But your chair creaks. How will you carry out that particular stage business? Will you act fear? Don't for heaven's sake let me make a noise with the chair? No. You will in the circle of your creative consciousness set in motion the energy in your feet and knees by directing all your powers there and not looking around as is usually done according to the conventions of the stage, that is, in order to act fear, etc., etc. You concentrate ALL YOUR ATTEN-TION ON THAT PARTICULAR SECTION OF YOUR PROBLEM. You are searching intently for help inside you, and the entire audience is with you. For it too is intent on the same task as you, drawn into your circle by your intense concentration. You finally get up. Oh, what a relief! You have succeeded in getting up without making a noise. Your second problem is to move across the room noiselessly. How many times does one see actors on the stage in just such a position? What do they do? Why, they raise their shoulders, draw in their head, bend forward, step heavily on each foot in turn, rolling their eyes about the room — all of which, according to the hackneyed conceptions of the stage, ought to express agitation. But what have you, a student-actor, to do? You have to transfer ALL YOUR ATTENTION ON THEM, setting the rest of your body free: shoulders, arms, neck; your head, neck, and shoulders must be held up straight so that your head and back form one straight line . . . leaving your extremities absolutely free to move about; so that you can set them in motion at any moment without the slightest effort on your part, but simply by the force of your will. As soon as your entire attention is concentrated on the tips of your toes, you find it easy to manipulate them.

You stand on tiptoe, or move across part of the room. Make up your mind beforehand where your place of refuge is to be, if the door is suddenly to be opened, so as not to look like a man caught in the act, etc. Your way across the room leads you to a small dressing table, but your real aim is your cigarette box on your desk. You tiptoe gently and effortlessly to your dressing table. You reach it without mishap. Your box is within your reach. Should you go on tiptoeing as before? No, etc., etc. Having reached the table, you start humming a tune, and so forgetting the door leading to the next room, etc., etc.

In addition to the relaxation of the muscles and the concentration on an object, Stanislavsky then included among the elements of the actor's psychotechnique an element whose main function is to arouse inspiration. This element is emotional memory — that is, memory which resides in the actor's feelings and is brought to the surface of his consciousness by his five senses, though Stanislavsky seemed to stress mostly sight and hearing.

Stanislavsky illustrated the meaning of emotional memory by asking an actor to imagine a large number of houses, large numbers of rooms in each house, a large number of cupboards in each room, drawers in each cupboard, large and small boxes in each drawer, and among the boxes, one that is very small and that is filled with beads. It is easy to find the house, the room, the cupboard, the drawer, the boxes, and even the smallest box of all. But it will take a very sharp eye to find the tiny bead that fell out of the box and, flashing for a moment, has gone for good. If it is found, it is by sheer accident. The same is true with the storehouse of an actor's memory. It too has its cupboards, drawers, and large and small boxes. Some of them are more and others less accessible. But how is the actor to find one of the beads of his emotional memory which flashed across his mind and then vanished, seemingly forever? Stanislavsky maintained that this is really the true task of the actors. This was the task I was to devote myself to in establishing the Method.

Stanislavsky went on to stress inner communication as one of the most important elements in acting. This is communication between the actor and his partner on stage, and between the actor and the audience. He differentiated the external movements of hand, feet, and trunk, which are visible to the eye, from those inner actions of spiritual communication, which are invisible to the eye, and which therefore seem inactive. Unfortunately, Stanislavsky, influenced by some of his previous interest in Hindu philosophy, kept describing this inner communication as "ray emission" and "ray absorption," as though the inner feelings and desires emitted rays which issued through the eyes and the body and poured in a stream over other people. He emphasized correctly that in his use of the five senses the actor must, if he listens, both listen and hear; if he smells, he must inhale; if he looks, he must look and see, not just glance at an object. But Stanislavsky was unable to describe his methods of mastering this process by suggesting exercises to facilitate ray emission and ray absorption.

These lectures delivered to the opera students and singers were the first concise presentation of Stanislavsky's system and are important as a presentation of his general ideas before the more systematic one in *An Actor Prepares* (1936). They agree very much with the ideas expressed in *My Life in Art* (1924), which tried to describe the way in which he arrived at his discoveries.

But Stanislavsky did not stop at this point: he continued to work to try to refine, define, and correct his ideas and to organize them into an understandable form so that they would not suffer the fate of most discoveries in the theatre and die with their creator.

We have already noted Stanislavsky's continuing dissatisfaction not with his ideas, but with his achievements. In addition, the static results obtained in some of the productions in which he had utilized his new methods led to continuous and recurring criticism of the actor's too-intense involvement with his own psyche, with insufficient outward expressiveness. Stanislavsky was not entirely upset by these criticisms since he agreed with some of them. He himself was not satisfied with the results, but they were important steps in his constant investigation of the actor's problem. He was more concerned with his failures in the classical repertoire, where, given the deepest and most intense experiences of the human soul, he had been unable to help the actors by means of all his methods to achieve the necessary depth of expression. He saw the work in the studios giving excellent results, but he was worried about the theatrical forms toward which they seemed to be leading. He was afraid that his work would become limited to modern, naturalistic plays.

Some of Stanislavsky's pupils, Vakhtangov and Nemirovitch-Dantchenko, seemed to be succeeding in those areas of heightened expressiveness where Stanislavsky himself had failed. In the early 1920s, Vakhtangov's productions of *The Dybbuk* and *Turandot,* with their theatricality, movement, and dynamics, must have drawn Stanislavsky's attention to elements other than the purely psychological. The brilliant productions by Nemirovitch-Dantchenko's musical studio, with their emphasis on rhythm and musicality and their success with the public, were something for Stanislavsky to envy, but they also demanded a rethinking of his system in the area of the expressiveness and embodiment of a character.

Stanislavsky was the great pioneer in the development of a system for the actor. But as we have seen, his work did not go far enough in solving the problem of expressiveness. His pupil Vakhtangov and his later follower Boleslavsky seemed to advance the actor's understanding of that problem. There are basic similarities in all three approaches an actor can take: representation, experience, and mechanical skill. Each follows the basic teachings Stanislavsky set out: the conscious training of the senses, leading to the unconscious creative means. This training of the technique of the actor consisted of a number of practical exercises in relaxation, concentration on objects, the circle of attention, etc. But what was most important was the use of the soul of the actor as the material for his work — the necessity for the study of the emotions and the analysis of simple and complicated feelings.

THE AMERICAN LABORATORY
THEATRE

THE work of Stanislavsky and the Moscow Art Theatre
had convinced me that acting was the process of living
on the stage. All my observations, all my knowledge, and
all my reading had led me to the right ideas. But the
ultimate question remained: How do you accomplish all
this? How do you bring alive the things you perceive?

I was to begin finding the answers at the American
Laboratory Theatre, run by Richard Boleslavsky and
Maria Ouspenskaya. It was located at 139 Macdougal
Street right next to the Provincetown Playhouse, which,
because of its association with O'Neill, has remained for
me the birthplace of the modern American theatre.

I entered the Laboratory Theatre with a great willing-
ness to absorb, but with little knowledge of what it was to
be. To be accepted into the Laboratory Theatre, one had
to pass a three-part audition. The first part was what might
be called a pantomimed exercise (actually one in sense
memory) in which you were asked to handle an imaginary
object. The second part consisted of creating an improvi-

sation with an older student. The subject of my improvisation was having to borrow money — a situation which, due to my financial condition at the time, was not too difficult for me to imagine. The third part of the audition involved memorizing and performing a speech from Shakespeare. I believe my speech was one of Shylock's from *The Merchant of Venice*. I must have passed my audition because I was invited to join. I was asked whether I could afford to pay or whether I required a scholarship. I declared that I had enough money for the year, and wished to pay. Thus began my life in the theatre.

I had seen both Richard Boleslavsky and Maria Ouspenskaya perform with the Moscow Art Theatre. In fact, I had seen Boleslavsky substitute for Stanislavsky in a one-act comedy. He had not impressed me very much as an actor, but I knew that he had been one of the original directors, along with Eugene Vakhtangov, of the Moscow Art Theatre Studio. I had been particularly impressed by Madame Ouspenskaya and her brilliant characterization of the governess in *The Cherry Orchard*. Ouspenskaya, one of the younger members of the Moscow Art Theatre, had been trained in the studio before she became a regular member of the company.

I remember the emotion of those first days at the Laboratory Theatre very well — it was almost a sense of revelation. I can vividly recall sitting there at the first sessions at the school, writing notes on what I heard, and thinking, "This is it. This is what it really means. This is what it is all about." The notes are a precise but cryptic documentation of what we were told and the exercises we participated in. They also contain my own comments on what we were being taught. As I look back over them, they show that my mind was active in assimilating and interpreting the teachings, but there is not a word about my own feeling and excitement. Oddly enough, my notes from those early sessions reflect none of my strange exhilaration.

My notebook indicates that on Tuesday, January 13, 1924 (two days before the premiere of Max Reinhardt's spectacular production of *The Miracle*), Boleslavsky defined for us the three different paths of theatre. The first one, which Boleslavsky called the commercial theatre, directed itself to financial or critical success through any means. In commercial theatre, the actor works to please the audience, remembering only not to speak too softly or too slowly. Everything else is copied from already successful patterns. I wrote the following notes from the lecture:[*]

Type system. Casting by looks, not by inward soul. . . . No chance for the actor to grow because always copying. 75% of great art is hard work — only about twenty-five percent is great talent. Bernhardt thrown out of the conservatory — not talented. Edmund Kean considered merely an acrobat. Talent only as a result of hard work.

The second path of theatre was what Boleslavsky called the French school. The French school historically started at a time when Greek and Roman writings were resurrected. The French school is more or less a copy of supposed classical theatre. The aim is to establish on stage classical mood, emotion, and so forth. The training of the actor aims at reaching a perfection in technical capabilities. The actor is absolutely conscious of what he is doing. Boleslavsky said, "They can surprise and astonish you, but never reach your soul."

The third path of theatre was the one that Boleslavsky

---

[*] All quotes are from a notebook Lee Strasberg kept from January 13, 1924, through January 30, 1925. It is in the Lee Strasberg collection. — Ed.

represented. He emphasized that it was not just a Russian school; art is universal and so are its principles. In my notebook I cite Boleslavsky's ideas:

> The main point of this School is that it is not enough to live through a part only once, and then represent it many times. The actor must live it through every time. In addition to the technical means of the actor (voice, speech, body) attention is put on the technique of feelings, and the feelings are never dissociated from the outer technique; they are used in every performance.

Boleslavsky emphasized that every feeling can be built up and trained.

In addition to the work on the actor's craft, Boleslavsky emphasized that this third path of theatre recognized the significance of the ensemble — of collective work. This work creates special results which you can find nowhere else. In every collective work, the important feature is that you must have a leader, but everything should be done by the group. Boleslavsky used the example of a rowing crew. They are directed by the coxswain, but all begin and work together. This example was contrasted to the work of an architect who, once he has finished his plans, is through. He then turns over the work to others to complete. These workers do not share the architect's initial creative feeling. The architect is not present during the realization of the work of art.

The vital significance of Boleslavsky's presentation of the three paths of theatre was that it separated the styles of theatre, and for that matter, even styles of acting, from the basic creative problems of the actor. In describing the procedures of the actor's work, Boleslavsky had presented the actor's problem not simply as deriving from the deficiencies of any individual; nor did he view the actor's problem as deriving from the contemporary realistic style, which demanded that the actor present as believable and real an image on stage as possible. Rather, Boleslavsky saw the problem of the actor as a basic, recurrent problem in the history of the theatre.

Equally important was the implicit recognition that not just the actor's technical means — his voice, speech, bodily actions — could be trained. Boleslavsky contended that the actor's internal means — what was still at that time called "soul" — could be trained. There were concrete methods or exercises that dealt with the most difficult aspects of the actor's work, such as imagination, emotion, and inspiration. The means of arriving at the actor's imagination, emotion, and inspiration were through concentration and affective memory.

I was first introduced to these techniques in those extraordinary classes at the American Laboratory Theatre. On the first day of classes, Madame Ouspenskaya introduced us to two exercises which demonstrated the general value of concentration. Madame (as we had been asked to call her) asked a number of us to get up and walk around. It was clear that we were uneasy, awkward, and uncomfortable; many glanced sideways at their fellow students, or at Madame, or at those watching to see if they could discern some sign that they were doing the correct thing. Even those affecting a false confidence by walking deliberately and precisely shared the same uneasiness.

Then Madame told us to move some books from one place to another and while we were walking, to think about something, to try to remember something: how many movies we had seen in the last year, who was in them, what the movie was about, who directed it. As we resumed walking, something strange took place. The walk became more natural, the rhythm less self-conscious. Everyone felt more comfortable when trying to remember. Something specific Madame told us: "Always have a reason, a problem, a cause for appearing on the stage."*

Vakhtangov had told his actors that at times it does not really matter what you think as long as you are thinking about something, something real. The important thing is, as we will have occasion to see later, not that what the actor deals with is an exact parallel to the play or the character, but that when the character thinks, the actor really thinks; when the character experiences, the actor really experiences — something. Whatever the actor does is modified not only by his intention, but by the nature and intensity of what is actually happening to him.

In the second exercise, Madame further illustrated the process of concentration with an exercise presumably taken from Indian or Eastern Yoga. The actor was instructed to take an object, say a matchbox, and examine it for five minutes, noticing everything about it: the exact size, the precise shape, the colors, the lettering on it, how far from the edge the lettering starts, the size and shape of the lettering, and so forth. Then he was to wait three minutes after his observation and write down what he remembered. That first day, the actor was surprised to see how much he had forgotten or not observed. The next time, he had to notice the material that the matchbox was made of, the material of the matches, what he knew about the making of wood matches, the discovery of fire, where matches were first used. In regard to the lettering and the coloring, he was to observe the artistic organization of it, the role of writing, and so forth. This little matchbox

---

* Directing this exercise on later occasions, I have made sure that the actor is truly thinking about something, instead of only pretending to think. Frequently, a young actor will knot his brow, press his lips, let his eyes flicker up or down or sideways as if he is thinking. When you question him, he isn't thinking about anything, he's just imitating the process of thinking.

became an image of the entire history of man. Thus, everything the actor looked at, when properly observed, could become much more important than its functional value in daily life. I don't remember that we ever actually did this exercise again after the first day, but it was quite easy to see its value and the point Madame was trying to emphasize. It is an exercise of enormous value for the actor: he must be able to perceive the significance of the details which the author describes or the words he has him speak. Many actors lose the value of much that is in the script only because they never relate to the specific object or reality that the words describe.

The central emphasis in the system set forth by Boleslavsky was on concentration and affective memory. Boleslavsky described the way in which these two elements are connected for the actor: "What you are doing on stage is the most important thing in the world at the present moment; and your memory must tell you how it is to be done."

According to Boleslavsky, affective memory falls into two categories: analytic memory, which recalls how something should be done; and the memory of real feeling, which helps the actor accomplish it on stage. Boleslavsky explained to us how the actor uses affective memory in developing a character: "The aim of affective memory is not really to feel or see or touch something — that is hallucination — but to remember the mood when doing that." (Notebook, January 23, 1925)

(I should note that the term *affective memory* was used unclearly at the American Laboratory Theatre. Perhaps because Boleslavsky and Madame were untrained in English, some confusion resulted in how they distinguished between the two categories of affective memory. In my own work, I divide affective memory into sense memory, which is the memory of physical sensation, and emotional memory, which is the memory of the experience of more intense responses and reactions. I will discuss these in a later chapter on my own discoveries.)

The exercises I describe here that we did at the American Laboratory Theatre deal only with the first part of affective memory — what Boleslavsky called analytic memory. Our work in this area was primarily with imaginary objects (or what Stanislavsky called "objects in the air") and imaginary events on stage. These would appear real and come alive on stage if the actor had been trained in stimulating the senses to actually respond to these objects. It should be emphasized that only the object is imaginary; the response is real.

When one reacts with an imaginary object, the response is exactly the same as if the object were not imaginary. Often, in everyday life, we recognize a person from afar and respond to him sympathetically or antagonistically depending on our relationship to him. Later, we learn that we made a mistake, that the individual was not who we thought he was; it is at that moment that we say, "I thought," or "I imagined," to differentiate from literal reality. But the actual response at the moment that we "thought" was completely equivalent to what it would have been if the person were the real one we took him for.

Both Stanislavsky and his great pupil Vakhtangov emphasized that literal reality is often not within the control of the actor. Only imaginary reality can be both created and, therefore, controlled by the actor. Beginning with objects that are in his daily environment, and by training to recreate them mentally, the actor strengthens his imagination. The task is for the actor to keep his attention centered on what he is doing, and to create the reality and truthfulness of each imaginary object or experience.

For the actor to achieve this, training had to begin with the five senses — sight, hearing, touch, taste, and smell —

plus the kinesic, or motor, senses. The training of the senses was a vital part of the conscious training of the actor. All human responses are the result of sensory experience. If we do not see the lion behind us, we will not react. If we do not hear the approaching train, we will not get off the tracks. If we do not hear an explosion, we are not startled. For any reaction to occur, the sense must function. The form that the reaction takes is differentiated by additional elements that shape the behavior. But without the senses, there is no life.

The training of the senses to respond to imaginary stimuli becomes part of the basic training of the actor; and the possession of this capacity to respond to imaginary stimuli is what characterizes the nature of the actor's talent. It is this that we look for to determine the presence of acting talent. All human beings respond to the presence of actual objects. Boleslavsky illustrated this point with an example: if a mouse accidentally wanders into a populated area, we see some of the finest acting that human beings are capable of. The ability to maintain that same response without the presence of that literal object is what constitutes the presence of imagination.

At the Laboratory Theatre, training involved a number of exercises in affective memory. For these exercises, each student was assigned an older student, called a shepherd, to assist him. We were introduced to many individual exercises involving imaginary objects — drinking tea, eating a grapefruit, putting on and taking off shoes and stockings. We had to differentiate between picking up pearls, nuts, potatoes, cantaloupes, and watermelons. In other exercises, my shepherd would ask me to see a picture on the wall, hear a certain noise, and so forth. These exercises, too, were designed to train the five primary senses.

I then worked with my shepherd on an exercise that

involved two simultaneous actions of affective memory. I was to drink a cup of tea and read a letter at the same time. One of the actions — drinking the tea — was to be entirely unconscious; my attention was to be wholly centered on the letter.

I have notes on another exercise I performed for Madame that involved imaginary objects. I was to come into a room and find my papers scattered on the floor by the open window. Some of them had become glued together, and I was supposed to pick them up and deal with them. In picking up some of the glued papers I tried to show resentment and disappointment. Madame told me: "No, now you are explaining to us what you feel; 'I am feeling so and so,' and in order to do that you make some movements of your face — don't do that. You just get the affective memory, really feel it, and we'll understand without your telling us, either by words or gestures." (Undated entry)

In an exercise involving an imaginary situation, I was to pass the half-open cage of a lion without arousing the animal. My notes indicate that Madame's general criticism was that I tried to show the fear I felt of the lion, instead of trying to pass him silently. "Instead realize that the only way to get out is to pass silently, and really try not to make any noise," Madame had told me. The notes of my own personal criticism of my exercise were that "I did get the connection with the imaginary object, but that when the lion noticed me, my behavior (rhythm) did not change." (February 6, 1925)

Madame conducted an exercise in which she emphasized real feeling over the demonstration of feeling. This was an interesting group exercise. We were to be a group of children awaiting the arrival of a favorite aunt, who was coming by boat. Madame would call off the arrival time — five minutes, four minutes, and so forth. Then, an announcement was made that the boat would be four hours late. Madame would caution us: "Don't try to act or show disappointment. Try to realize what is really being said and what it means. Don't show the result of the moment instead of living through the moment. Don't act the moment, just take time to realize what it means to you, that's all." (February 6, 1925) We were to place our emphasis on our effort to see the boat, to see the other objects around us.

On a later occasion, the exercise was amplified. As we saw the boat draw close, it would suddenly explode. The entire attention of the actor is to focus on the objects and on the events that happen; not to worry about the emotion.

It is sometimes assumed even by some who agree with this approach as a basis for the actor's training that its purpose is to help the actor react to real objects on the stage. Therefore, some prefer to use actual objects in the process of training, believing that this will help the actor to become more expert. This is quite true and useful, but it negates the primary value of this type of training as emphasized by both Stanislavsky and my own teachers. The handling of real objects on the stage does not train the actor to solve the problem of the stage experience. Thus, although one has put on stockings every day, it is quite a different matter to do the same thing on stage under imaginative circumstances.

The purpose of affective memory training for Boleslavsky was not simply to help the actor become more adept at handling props which he will have to deal with on the stage, but more essentially to train and develop the actor's imagination so that he can deal with the nonexistent reality which is the primary characteristic of the stage. He will be given literal props to use in performance, but he can never have use of a real murder to respond to, of a real ghost to help him represent Hamlet's confrontation with that of his father, of a real knife floating in the air that summons Macbeth to his task, of the blood Lady Macbeth tries to get rid of throughout her sleepwalking scene — not to mention the difficulty of creating the sleepwalking itself.

Boleslavsky had devised a number of animal exercises for us to work on. Like the affective memory work, these were designed to strengthen the actor's imagination. In one class we had to perform various activities while behaving like monkeys, elephants, horses, squirrels, etc. I participated in one exercise where all the students were tigers. My notes indicate that Madame said I had achieved the restless movement of the tiger, but not the inner feeling: "Do not only imitate the tiger," I was told, "but try to feel what the tiger feels. See the bars of your cage, feel the unrest." (February 6, 1925)

These animal exercises had a significant intention. Madame explained that they were designed to make the actor "look for some elements necessary to characterize and realize the animal." Actors have a tendency to approach any part with the assumption that they resemble that character. Often they leave out an important part of their characterization because they do not perceive the difference between themselves and the character. My notes indicate that she went on to say: "In approaching the animal exercises, the actor is made aware that he is not the animal, and therefore immediately begins to try to discover and investigate what behavior characterizes that particular animal." (February 6, 1925)

The actor's behavior in these exercises is not only a matter of neuromuscular activity, but as was already suggested by Madame, "of the sensory and at times the emotional response of the animal." Here, too, the importance of the exercise lies not in the immediate results, but in the more fundamental demands that are made upon the actor's imagination.

From the animal exercises we moved to other group exercises that involved the presentation of characters foreign to our own personalities. In my notes of January 24, 1924, I describe one of these exercises:

We had to be Indians with the problem of presenting something to the New England farmers who were celebrating Christmas. The results were not good. Always pick out something characteristic. Indian placing one foot in other's tracks. The farmer's physical vigor which would have made us dance till we were warm. It happened to be a very cold day.

Our exercises with Boleslavsky and Madame were confined to the area of analytic memory. They were designed to train the actor's imagination. It was later in my own work with the problems of the actor that exercises dealing with "emotional memory" were developed.

Besides concentration and affective memory, there was an additional element in the Laboratory's approach to the actor's training: action.

Action is not a literal paraphrase of the author's words, nor a synonym for what transpires on the stage, nor a logical analysis of the scene. Action has always been *the* essential element in the theatre. The very word *actor* implies that. Every actor makes use of one or another kind of action.

The external actor thinks of it as the "stage business" of his role: where he moves, where he sits, where and how he reacts, where he emphasizes a thought by suspending some physical act. All of this is a means of suggesting what the character is thinking, feeling, or doing.

In addition to that, every actor creates a sequence of actions which are a physical routine: he comes in the door, he stops, sighs, looks around, takes off his jacket, rolls up his sleeves, and performs some daily activity — something that he is accustomed to being concerned with while he speaks the lines of the character. These physical actions often create an imitation of, an indication of, what the character is doing.

Yet even in this area of stage business, true actions should be accomplished with the help of the senses and concentration. To repeat, when the character stops and is thinking of what he is going to do, the actor must really think, not only pretend to think. Maybē he expected to find someone at home who is not there; or, he is thinking of how he should approach his next task, which may involve the delivery of some special news. Yet these physical routines may be done while his mind and his experience are involved in some other basic task which is truly the action of the scene.

The real action of the scene is expressed by the character's intentions. Let us imagine a scene with just a few lines:

Someone comes in a door. A female voice calls off stage, "Are you home, darling?"

He answers, "Yes."

The off-stage voice continues, "How was the day?"

He answers, "Fine."

The voice goes on to ask, "Are you ready to have dinner?"

He responds, "Mmmm."

Now the man may be coming home because he has been fired and must share the news with his wife. That becomes his action and will often direct his behavior long before the actual dialogue permits the expression of it; or, the man may think he has discovered something suspicious about his wife and comes in to find out whether it is true. The physical actions remain practically the same, but the way in which they are accomplished depends upon the emotional action of the scene: how will he go about it? Should he do it right away? And so on. All these actions with the same general physical pattern of movement would result in quite different behavior on the part of the actor.

Actions, to be of any value, must suggest something that the words themselves do not necessarily imply. Actions are not simply physical or mental, but physical, motivational, and emotional. For instance, Gordon Craig described the action which pervades the entire play of *Hamlet* as being "the search for the truth." While he himself never clearly described how it would affect the acting of the role, it definitely influenced his own visual conception of the production. Under Stanislavsky's direction, Craig produced and advised the Moscow Art Theatre's 1912 production. In the first scene in the court, the entire ensemble, including the king and queen, seemed to be poured out of molten gold. In actuality, a golden cloth covered the entire stage, and the heads of the characters appeared through it. Hamlet sat at the side in front, so that the court appeared almost as an image in his mind of the way in which he sees it. Because of the basic action — the search for the truth — the costumes for the players made them appear almost like winged creatures of the imagination. That was because to Craig the players represented a higher truth.

The whole play seen from this action becomes unified by Hamlet's need to find out, to discover, to resolve his doubts and uncertainties about the declarations of the ghost; when he does so, he is quite resolute and definite in his behavior. Hamlet derived the idea for testing the king from the first player's speech. The "To be or not to be" speech becomes not simply a moody soliloquy or a hysterical expression of a desire to commit suicide, but a search for what one should do to arrive at the truth of human life.[*]

As important as action is, it comes into play only after the actor has been trained to respond and to experience. Action then becomes the means by which the actor enters the realm of what the play deals with. A play is a sequence of various kinds of action. These in turn derive from the given circumstances of the scene, that is, those events and experiences which motivate the actor to do what he comes on stage to achieve.[†]

Even more than the individual psychological and physical exercises at the Laboratory Theatre, it was Boleslavsky's notion of a unified system of actor training that remained with me. Vocal training, relaxation, movement

---

[*] Francis Fergusson, who studied at the Laboratory, described Boleslavsky's concept of action in the following way:

> The "dramatic action" of a play or of a part is always expressed by an infinitive. For instance, the "action" of Chekhov's *The Three Sisters* has been called "to get to Moscow." . . . The "action" of Oedipus in *Oedipus the King* is not the story which is unfolded in the course of the play, but "to get at the cause of the city's woes" — a movement which reaches its completion in the full revelation of his guilt. As for the "action" of this play — each play as well as each role has an action — that is very hard to find in a masterpiece of a remote epoch, but the quest is very fruitful.

The action Fergusson describes in *The Three Sisters,* "to get to Moscow," hardly succeeds in being more than a paraphrase of the words and would be of little use to an actor. In fact, there are times in some unfortunate productions that I have seen where, when the sisters continue to express their desire to get to Moscow, as if that were what the play was about, the audience has almost audibly responded, "I wish they would stop complaining and go there already."

[†] Although Stanislavsky himself always stressed that actions were psychophysical, there is a great confusion and misunderstanding of even such a simple term as *action*. The unfortunate formulation of Stanislavsky's ideas as the "theory or method of physical actions" is based on later writings, which must always be seen in conjunction with Stanislavsky's earlier discoveries. Some "experts" who rely only on this later work assume that the concept of action had been previously unknown to us at the American Laboratory Theatre. These people have created elaborate imaginary theories about the differences between the way in which I received an understanding of Stanislavsky's technique and their own later formulations.

Lee Strasberg at his graduation from Hebrew High School.

A performance of The Man Who Married a Dumb Wife *at the Chrystie Street Settlement House, 1927.*

Tommaso Salvini, "The Famous Italian Trage-dian, One of the Greatest Modern Exponents of the Character of Othello," c. 1887.

Giovanni Grasso. Lee Strasberg's program from the performance at the Grand Street Theatre, 1928.

Sketch by Edward Gordon Craig for the Moscow Art Theatre's production of Hamlet.

Constantin Stanislavsky surrounded by Moskvin, Katchalov, Chaliapin, and Sorin. The painting in the background is of Anna Pavlova.

Cover of the souvenir program of the Moscow Art Theatre, 1923.

THE
RUSSIAN
PLAYERS

IN AMERICA

THE·MOSCOW·ART·THEATRE
BALIEFF'S·CHAUVE·SOURIS

TEXT WRITTEN BY
OLIVER M. SAYLER

TEXT AND PICTURES
ETCHED ON COPPER
BY
BERNHARDT·WALL

COPYRIGHT 1923
BERNHARDT WALL
NEW YORK CITY

Constantin Stanislavsky, "Co-Founder and First Artist of the Moscow Art Theatre," 1923.

Vladimir Nemirovitch-Dantchenko, "Co-Founder of the Moscow Art Theatre," 1923.

Lee Strasberg, c. 1931.

Paula Miller Strasberg and J. Edward Bromberg in a Group Theatre production. (Vandamm Studio, the Billy Rose Theatre Collection, New York Public Library)

The founders of the Group Theatre: Lee Strasberg, Harold Clurman, and Cheryl Crawford.

Lee Strasberg (seated, extreme right) conducting a rehearsal with the members of the Group Theatre. (Clifford Odets is standing with a script in his hand.)

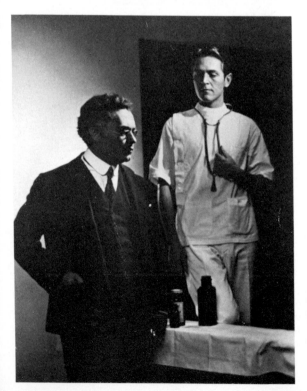

J. Edward Bromberg and Alexander Kirkland in Sidney Kingsley's Men White, *directed by Lee Strasberg, 1933.*

Lee Strasberg (far right, standing) in the Group Theatre's production of Till the Day
I Die, *by Clifford Odets, 1935. This was his last performance on Broadway.*

...cene from Johnny Johnson, *by Paul Green and Kurt Weill, 1936. This was the last play
...asberg directed for the Group Theatre.*

Lee Strasberg as he so often was seen: with a book, listening to music, 1936.

Lee Strasberg (right) in discussion after a rehearsal, 1940.

work, affective memory études — all these components are essential for the schooling of the actor. Yet more electrifying was the growing concept set forth by Boleslavsky of a fixed sequence of procedures that would serve the young actor in the same way standard training techniques serve the young musician — a sequence of exercises that would physically and mentally develop the necessary stimulus for creativity in the actor.

Those of us who were beginning students were permitted to attend the special lecture Boleslavsky conducted for his advanced group on January 30, 1925. It was the beginning of the second stage of their training and dealt with learning to control even their most inspired moments. Up until now, the training had consisted of attaining unconscious control through conscious preparation. But here, Boleslavsky was dealing directly with the paradox posed by Diderot. I recorded his comments in my notebook.

The preparation of every art must be conscious — you must know how and what you are going to do. Don't trust your inspiration . . . but look to your own conscious understanding of what you are going to do. Then being trained in the method do to the best of your ability — this factor of ability must be unconscious. Conscious preparation — unconscious result. This unconsciousness in performing, in projecting the part, is the most precious moment of the play. It is not mere forgetfulness, due to tiredness, or, on the other hand, hallucination; but the prompting of artistic fire. But this is only the first stage or floor of unconsciousness. We must develop a second floor of unconsciousness. In order to give you control of your unconscious moments and train your unconscious memory, exercise. Give yourself a conscious problem:

hammer a nail into the wall. Now, do the action unconsciously, but remember just how and what you did,
i.e., what your *body* did, what the *action* is. That is the
soul of the problem. Remember why you went to hammer the nail — to hang yourself on it? Or hang a
picture of your sweetheart? Remember the energy,
i.e., the rhythm of your action — are you tired or not?
Do not try to watch yourself and see what you are
doing, but try to feel just how and what you did. [*In
other words, utilizing sensory memory. — L.S. later addition*]
To give unconscious adjustment to surroundings and
to all that others are doing, use the same problem
hammering nail under the craziest situations and let
the actor adjust himself to it. [*You try not to awaken
anybody. You must not be caught. You are fleeing from
someone, and so on. — L.S. later addition*] Then use an
unconscious adjustment or try listening to the audience. This cannot be explained, you merely feel it.
Practice two or three minutes of concentration every
day, and three minutes of unconscious adjustment.

Boleslavsky then sketched this drawing for us which
appears opposite.* The ground floor shows the conscious
preparation for the unconscious result. The second floor
represents the additional adjustment that characterizes
what the actor is creating: body, action, and energy;
adjustment to surroundings; and adjustments to the audience. That leads to the attic, which he nicknamed the
"crazy house." On top, there were two chimneys belching
smoke — they represented "Praise" and "Glory." Boleslavsky's explanation of the progress the actor makes
through the "house" formed the basis of the ideas I was to
begin to develop at the Group Theatre.

* Spelling is Strasberg's. — Ed.

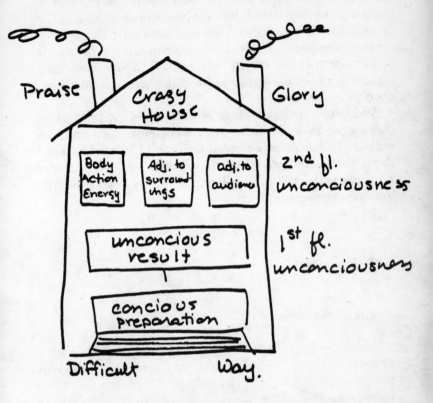

Attending the Laboratory Theatre school at the same time that I did were individuals of the calibre of John Martin, who became the outstanding dance critic of the *New York Times;* Francis Fergusson, who developed into a respected professor of comparative literature; Harold Hecht, who graduated into the ranks of Hollywood producers; George Auerbach, who became a film director; Stella Adler, who was an actress on the Yiddish stage and who, in the days of the Group Theatre, became a highly respected American actress destined for greatness. Yet none of them found that all-consuming interest in the process of acting that I felt. Harold Clurman in his *The Fervent Years* characterized me as "fanatic on the subject of true emotion." While I am perhaps not a fanatic, I must admit I feel as intensely today about the basic discoveries of Stanislavsky as I did then. And if anything, even more so.

And while the importance and the need for relaxation, concentration, and affective memory (sense and emotional memory) were already clear at the time I first encountered them early in 1924, they have taken on even greater meaning and significance during my many years of search and experience since then.

THE VOYAGE CONTINUES: I
Discoveries at the Group Theatre

I have tried in my analysis of Stanislavsky's discoveries, and in the description of my own experiences at the Laboratory Theatre, to emphasize that the purpose of the actor's training — the exercises designed to develop the imagination and train belief on the stage — are intended to help the actor create the necessary reality demanded by the play. All of this training deals with the actor's process of creation. But the actor must also be able to express the reality which his conscious or unconscious technique helps him to discover. Stanislavsky was well aware of this actor's problem of expression — that is, what the actor conveys to the audience. This is why he divided his book *The Actor Works on Himself** into two parts, the first dealing with the actor's work on himself in the process of creation or rehearsal; and the second, with the actor's work on himself in the process of embodiment or expression in performance. Stanislavsky himself expressed concern and dissat

---

* It is better known in English as *An Actor Prepares*.

isfaction at his inability to achieve the desired results of expression, especially in classical plays. His outstanding student Eugene Vakhtangov, while making use of his master's procedures, had already revised some of Stanislavsky's formulations. These changes helped Vakhtangov achieve the startling and highly theatrical results upon which his fame rests.

My understanding of Stanislavsky's work had come through the representation of his ideas which I first received at the Laboratory Theatre. Through my teachers there, Maria Ouspenskaya and Richard Boleslavsky, I learned the principles of the Stanislavsky system.

I have often been asked what the relation is between the "Stanislavsky system" and what is commonly called "the Method." I have always stated simply that the Method was based on the principles and procedures of the Stanislavsky system. I began to use these principles in the early thirties, training and working with young actors in the Group Theatre, and then later in my own classes and at the Actors Studio. However, I have always referred to our own work as a "method of work," because I never liked the implication of the term *system*. Additionally, in view of the many discussions and misunderstandings as to what "the system" is and what it is not, plus the confusion about the earlier and later periods of Stanislavsky's work, I was unwilling to make Stanislavsky responsible for any of our faults.

The work which I represent can now legitimately be called the Method. It is based not only on the procedures of Stanislavsky's work, but also on the further clarification and stimulus provided by Vakhtangov. I have also added my own interpretation and procedures. Through our understanding, analysis, applications, and additions, we have made a sizable contribution to the completion of Stanislavsky's work. My own discoveries at the Group Theatre, at the Actors Studio, and in my private classes arrive at answers for the problems of expression.

The Method is, therefore, the summation of the work that has been done on the actor's problem for the last eighty years. I bear a certain degree of responsibility for it and can now speak of it with some degree of authority. My own part was in developing, training, and directing the ensemble of the Group Theatre. Here we applied the procedures of the Method to a complete theatre unit. Since 1948, as the artistic director of the Actors Studio and in my private classes, we have tried to apply the work to the individual actor. In the following chapters, I intend to describe the additional discoveries and procedures which my experiences have contributed over the years.

One of my chief discoveries as the director of the Group Theatre was a reformulation of Stanislavsky's "creative if." As I mentioned earlier, Stanislavsky's formulation of the "creative if" consists of the proposition, Given the particular circumstances of the play, how would you behave, what would you do, how would you feel, how would you react? Whereas this is suitable in plays close to the contemporary and psychological experience of the actor, it fails to help the actor attain the necessary intense and heroic behavior that is characteristic of the great classical plays. Vakhtangov, who was committed to the search for a more definite theatrical intention and form, reformulated Stanislavsky's proposition in the following manner: The circumstances of the scene indicate that the character must behave in a particular way; what would motivate you, the actor, to behave in that particular way?

In the early productions of the Group Theatre, I, too, found that Stanislavsky's formulation of the "creative if" proved unsatisfactory in dealing with a variety of problems involving our plays and our actors. I therefore utilized

Vakhtangov's reformulation in actual practice. It seemed to me correct, both in terms of dealing with the problems of our productions, and in solving some of the limitations Stanislavsky himself had acknowledged.

The reformulation not only requires the actor to create the desired artistic result, but demands that he make it real and personal to himself in order to achieve it. This involves the principles of motivation and substitution. The actor is not limited to the way in which he would behave within the particular circumstances set for the character; rather, he seeks a substitute reality different from that set forth by the play that will help him to behave truthfully according to the demands of the role. It is not necessarily the way he himself would behave under the same circumstances, and thus does not limit him to his own natural behavior.

The work in the Group Theatre that created difficulties and confusion with some of the actors stemmed from my unwillingness as a director to accept the actor's own natural behavior in that set of circumstances dictated by the play. Rather, I was intent upon searching for adjustments and conditions not necessarily related to the play, but still coming from the actor's own experience. Only that, I felt, would create the desired result on stage.

It has often been assumed that the actor should be thinking exactly what the character is thinking. Many actors who disagree with this approach have, sometimes when they were complimented on a particular moment, gleefully responded, "Aha, so you thought it was good, huh? Do you know what I was thinking about at that moment?" They then go on to describe something completely extraneous to what the character should have been concerned with: where to have dinner, when to do the laundry, etc. But the important thing is that they were thinking about something real and concrete rather than the make-believe thinking which that same actor would usually perform.

I am always surprised by how little is known of our actual training and rehearsal procedures in the Group Theatre. Perhaps a few examples of how these adjustments or substitutions were brought into productions would explain how my reformulation of Stanislavsky's "creative if" worked.

In John Howard Lawson's *Success Story,* which I directed in 1932, Luther Adler was cast as a hot-tempered class-conscious stock boy who pushes his way to the top. The character was motivated by an all-encompassing anger at his class situation. Luther could not find the true emotion of his character. I told him we needed a reaction that showed his anger, but Luther had never felt a personal wrong in his life that had produced such a reaction. After some work in rehearsal, I finally asked him, "What makes you angry?" Luther replied, "When someone does something awful to someone else, I get furious." Luther therefore created a substitute situation in his own mind: a wrong done to someone close to him. This allowed him to produce the character's destructive energy. Of course, the audience was unaware of Luther's private motivation. All they saw was the true anger of the stock boy.

A more complicated adjustment was used in the same production of *Success Story.* Stella Adler, Luther's sister, had an unusual emotional intensity, expressiveness, and physical vitality that the playwright felt was wrong for the character of the meek Jewish secretary who was secretly in love with the stock boy. Lawson wanted Stella to play the role of the sensuous and glamorous wife of the corporation head. We perceived in Stella, however, the presence of the emotional colors needed to create a controlled but dynamic character. I wanted a deep emotion — which Stella had — but contained in a pure, lovely, ethereal quality. It was very difficult to get this from her because of her natural tendency to "burn up the stage." In one sequence, Stella's character was supposed to show concealed longing for the stock boy, but for Stella, the notion of a repressed, hidden, calm romance was alien to her own behavior. All of her attempts were overdone, or without any personal truth.

She was finally able to achieve the character by means of an unusual adjustment, which I called the "shipboard adjustment." I gave Stella the following instructions: "You are on a boat, alone, it's nighttime, moonlight. There's a man there, and you talk. But you know it's not going to last. And therefore you tell each other things that you would never tell anyone you know. You don't spill your guts to somebody you don't know, but you share it. You romance the other person, and on the fifth day, you say it's been very nice, let's meet again sometime, and you leave. It's very real. But it's pure, it doesn't seek anything else."

This adjustment worked for her. She was to think that everything on the stage was actually happening on the ship; she had to create and retain the sensation of being on board the ship: the moonlight, the water, the romantic mood. Thus, she brought nothing of the way she would behave in an office onto the stage. Not only did the adjustment work, but people came back stage and didn't recognize her. Friends told her that she was so different, so changed, so calm. It was probably her most distinguished performance.

One year after *Success Story*, the Group Theatre had its first artistic and financial triumph on Broadway with Sidney Kingsley's *Men in White*. This was really the first hospital drama. Joe Bromberg had been cast as the chief doctor. Bromberg, who had mainly been identified with comic parts, had a kind of joviality that did not seem at all suitable to the character. Bromberg had to develop a much more contained, much more mysterious, and much more assertive quality. I suggested what was called the "FBI adjustment." In it, I had him imagine that he was an FBI agent who had been sent to investigate the Group Theatre. He could not give away the fact that he was an FBI agent, nor could he tell any of the actors. As in the shipboard adjustment, this created a strange, new quality appropriate to the character.

We faced the problem of creating a group adjustment in *Gold Eagle Guy*, a play by Melvin Levy which I directed in 1939. An earthquake was to take place at the end of the second act, and the actors had to respond. In a real earthquake, the rumbling and chaos is followed by people running out of their homes to see what has happened. Scenically, however, I needed a sharp, vivid reaction to the event. I created an adjustment for the actors by telling them:

"You are escaping from one country into another." (At that time, refugees were fleeing Germany, so this situation was firmly imprinted in their minds.) "You have been smuggled into hiding places on the edge of the border. Tonight, you are locked up, and tomorrow you will be taken across the frontier. Suddenly, there is a fire."

I then created sensory cues for them that were triggered by lights: someone smells smoke, someone then realizes that their hideaway is on fire. Finally, people understand that they are trapped. The effect of the group's reaction was tremendous.

The purpose in each of these substitutions was never one of creating emotion per se, nor was it to create the emotion which the actor himself would naturally express in those circumstances. Rather, the purpose was to find a way of creating the emotional reaction demanded of the character by the text. Most of the Group actors achieved an excellence verified not just by myself, but by the critics and the audiences. But frequently they felt stifled, put upon, and confined in rehearsal. While I was able to sympathize, I could not agree with them. I could not accept the actor's mere expression of himself as being of service to the play.

The creation of emotion is in itself not always a problem (especially with actors as emotionally facile as Miss Adler). The creation of *the right kind* of emotion remains a continuing problem for the actor. The work done in this area under my direction at the Group Theatre opened possibilities and dimensions that were later to prove an important addition to the fundamentals put forth by Stanislavsky and Vakhtangov — not only in the actor's capacity to experience, but also in his capability to express that experience vividly and intensely. It helped to find a solution that leads the actor from creation to expression in ways that eschew purely external approaches.

In his story of the Group Theatre, *The Fervent Years*, Harold Clurman emphasized (unfortunately, without sufficient explanation) that improvisation and what I refer to as affective or emotional memory were the two areas that I was concerned with. There were, of course, others, as I have just discussed. But there is a certain justification in emphasizing these two. Certainly in the rehearsal process, I did place a great deal of emphasis on improvisation as it related to the creation of the ensemble. Regarding affective memory, I placed a great deal of emphasis on the actor's experience, which is essentially his memory of emotional moments — which even great actors are not always able to create at will.

Stanislavsky himself had never fully expounded the

procedures of improvisation, work w̶̶̶
and emotional memory. It is in the
Method has made a significant contribut̶
with the Group Theatre, most of the pr̶
applied within the context of rehearsing for
production.

The aim of these experiments with improvisation was to permit the actor, both in the process of training and in rehearsal, to develop the necessary flow of thought and sensation which leads to the development of spontaneity on stage. This spontaneity must encompass both the prepared actions and memorized lines, and also leave room for "the life of the moment." This creates in both the actor and the audience the sensation of something taking place here and now.

Improvisation leads to a process of thought and response and also helps the actor to discover the logical behavior of the character, rather than "merely illustrating" the obvious meaning of the line.

Another problem arose in terms of expression that required a heightened theatricality. While the Group actors were already known for their detailed realistic characterizations, we foresaw a special problem in dealing with heightened theatrical forms such as Shakespeare, commedia dell'arte, Molière, and musical comedy. The task was to create a procedure that would school the Group actors to perform in a stylized manner without the loss of inner justification and truthful motivation. Among the exercises we developed were those involving improvisations with objects (both real and imaginary), words, paintings, and improbable adjustments. These improvisations often led to an understanding of a heightened theatrical style. Some improvisations based on paintings by George Grosz were very successful, as was the work done famous operating room scene in *Men in White*. Most critics, in fact, characterized this scene as a "ballet." I will deal further with improvisation later on.

My own work, which provided the foundation of the training for the Group Theatre ensemble, veered from the intense psychological realism of *The House of Connelly* to a growing theatricality demonstrated in the productions of *1931*, *Success Story*, and *Men in White*, which were close in style to, but not as theatrically obvious as, the work of the Vakhtangov Theatre. Later, the musical play *Johnny Johnson*, which I directed, achieved an outright theatricality fitting the nature of the material. One critic characterized the work as being a mixture of Hogarth, the Marx Brothers, and Charlie Chaplin. The work of Harold Clurman in his Group Theatre productions seemed characterized by a psychological intensity, demonstrated in Clifford Odets's *Paradise Lost* and in the freer and more vivid realism of *Awake and Sing!* and *Golden Boy*. Robert Lewis's production of *My Heart's in the Highlands*, by William Saroyan, was an excellent example of fantasy realism and demonstrated a search for a stylized reality which continued to characterize his work in the theatre. Elia Kazan's work as a director, which started in the Group Theatre, was highly dynamic. But the demands of the material forced him to be essentially realistic, though there were signs of a heightened theatricality in some of his later productions, such as *JB* by Archibald MacLeish. The full scope of Kazan's theatrical vision as indicated in a projected production of a classic Greek play has never, unfortunately, been shared with the public.

The Group Theatre was not so much a period of discovery as it was a period of utilizing previous discoveries in the process of actual professional productions. The concern during this period was with practical application rather than theory. It was a way of testing what we had learned from the Stanislavsky system as presented by our own teachers; it was also an attempt to check our knowledge and our ability to use those principles to achieve our own results, without imitating what Stanislavsky and his other followers achieved.

THE VOYAGE CONTINUES: II
The Actors Studio and My Classes

WHEN I became the artistic director of the Actors Studio in 1948, I came to realize more and more that an actor could experience and yet not be able to express an emotion. I had always known about this problem and had dealt with it in the practical terms of production. But now, I was fully aware of this as a central problem in acting.

Shakespeare has Hamlet expound on the actor's effort to "force his soul so to his own conceit . . . and all for nothing! For Hecuba! . . . What would he do had he the motive and the cue for passion that I have?" The French director Jacques Copeau described this inability to find his "cue for passion" as "the actor's struggle with his own blood." This was the problem we set out to solve.

However, I was discovering something else: the actor could "struggle with his own blood" and find "the cue for passion," and yet somehow be unable to express it. This was something that had not been recognized throughout the history of our art! This difficulty in expressing oneself is true not only for actors, but for all human beings. I began to seek its sources.

It was not hard to discover them. Whatever capacities the human being is born with, it is by means of training and conditioning that he learns to use them. He learns to walk and talk without any awareness of the mechanisms that go into these procedures. He learns to make musical sounds without knowing what his throat has to do to achieve them. He learns to pronounce words without any awareness of the muscles and nerves that participate in that activity. It takes five years for a child to learn to put his shoes on and tie the laces. Once he has learned how to do it, he simply does it by habit. He develops habits of thought, of speech, of behavior, of attitudes toward his environment.

He also develops habits of expression. He is conditioned to express his feelings and emotions not by the nature, character, and strength of his own emotional responses, but by what society or his environment will permit. He is usually aware of his physical habits, but has little knowledge of his sensory and emotional reactions.

By the time an individual arrives at the age where he begins to aspire to be an actor, he is to some extent aware of his physical attributes, such as his voice, speech, and movement patterns. He has little or no knowledge of the strengths and weaknesses of his sensory and memory equipment; even less does he understand the behavior of his emotions and the way in which he expresses them.

Often he does so in ways which become so limited that we call them "mannerisms." Since to the individual these are his natural expressions, he thinks of them as being real and true and does not perceive that they are mannered. At the Actors Studio I had to find ways of dealing with an actor's mannerisms that obscured the truth of expression that involves the relationship between intensity of feeling and emotion.

In one instance I faced this problem with an actress of stature and great talent. She had a set of mannerisms that were the acquired characteristics of her conditioning. In one scene, she would constantly flutter her hands. To discourage this, we tied her hands behind one of the pillars that helped sustain the balcony. This forced her to eliminate the involuntary nervous behavior of her hands, and simply to wait until the need for organic expression arose. When the emotional motivation became strong enough, without thinking, she snapped the light thread that bound her hands behind the pillar. By then, the gesture was both necessary and fully expressive of the emotion behind it.

Another highly gifted young actress refused to recognize the difference between her mannerisms and her reality. It took her over ten years before she was able to accept the idea. Once she was able to acknowledge this, her acting showed remarkable progress.

It is striking the extent to which habits of expression are connected with the difficulties of expression. Often these difficulties derive from definite experiences that led to the creation of unconscious habits. Often these habits can be released during the part of the actor's training that involves relaxation.

An actress who worked with me at the Studio over an extensive period of time encountered unusual difficulty in relaxation. She was a professional actress and had made a career for herself in radio. Initially, she had a very negative attitude toward her work on stage because she relied on her verbal skills, but eventually she began to be able to create on the stage with much greater conviction and reality. She also became able to relax, which indicated a greater degree of will and control. Despite the progress, she still had trouble relaxing the back of her neck, an area of great mental tension for many people. Since her work was generally showing improvement, I became curious about the particular problem she was having. I tried to help her to put her head back far enough to rest on the back of the chair, in order to relax the nerves and muscles, which seemed somewhat rigid. She complained that she could not do so because she had arthritis. When she put her head back, she experienced a very sharp pain in her neck. To investigate, I supported her neck, encouraged her to let it rest in my hand, and asked her to tell me when the pain started. She had achieved a reasonable state of relaxation except for this particular area of her body. I kept moving the head back slowly, half an inch at a time, waiting for her to tell me when the pain started. The head finally reached the back of the chair and she had yet to exhibit any pain. She said she had not been able to move that area freely since she was a child. I found it difficult to conceive that she had been aware of tension in the crib. No, she stated. It was when she began to sleep in the bed. I asked her what happened when she began to sleep in the bed. She said that she slept with her older sister and, being a youngster, she moved around quite a good deal. Her sister had threatened to kill her if she didn't lie still. Since then she had developed rigidity, centered particularly in the neck. She then confided that while the doctors had checked her and determined that she had an arthritic condition, there seemed no reason for the degree of pain that she complained of. Obviously, both the tension and the pain were the result of conditioning. The release of those areas was essential for her to free herself from mannerisms and tension that interfered with her ability to express herself on stage.

In another instance, I came across what I learned to describe as an "oppositional stance" on the part of the actor. In the course of the relaxation work, when the actor seems in a relaxed attitude, I check to make sure that this is not simply an assumed attitude. I will lift the arm by lifting the hand. If the actor is really relaxed, as I let go of the hand, the arm falls naturally. If the arm is still tense, it remains in position up in the air. The actor then realizes that it is remaining there and lets it down mechanically. He is aware, however, that he is faking relaxation. With some people, even after the rest of the body has begun to relax, as I pick up the arm by the hand and try to let it go, the arm pulls in, although there is no indication of any unwillingness to let go. I have discovered that this usually suggests some built-in conditioning to oppose whatever is demanded. Regardless of whether the individual wishes to do something or is ordered to do something, the first reaction of his instrument (his body) to his will is one of opposition.

In a particular instance, an actress had exhibited good progress in her general relaxation, yet there were still areas of tension that exhibited themselves not only in the relaxation exercises, but in her acting as well. During one exercise, I lifted her arm; there was tension with some slight suggestion of the oppositional stance. I told her she was tense, expecting that she would make an effort to relax. She did not respond. I repeated my comment, and, to make sure that she heard and responded to me, I lightly hit the arm. Immediately she relaxed that area. Something made me say, "Did you use to be punished?"

She said, "Yes."

"A lot?"

"Yes."

"Were you very stubborn despite that?"

"Yes." That helped to explain both the degree of her tension and the rigidity of her neck and back muscles during relaxation. This is an area which some psychiatrists believe retains certain types of traumatic emotional experiences. No amount of physical exercise can correct these tensions. The area has to be approached through the connection between mind and body, a major aspect of most schools of modern psychology.

An example of a different kind serves to illustrate not only the role of habit, but the extent to which other experiences can decisively condition the behavior of an individual. A young actress had difficulties relaxing almost every area of her body. The legs, including the feet, were especially tense, which was unusual. As she began to be able to relax in some areas, the legs still demonstrated unusual resistance to a degree I had rarely observed before. She was performing an exercise in emotional memory, and I was trying to discover some possible reason for her unusual behavior — unusual from the technical point of view of the actor. There seemed to be something taking place while she was doing the exercise. In her acting in general, she often seemed to be in conflict or in contradiction with what she was trying to will herself to do. I tried to discover what it was that happened to her when she came on the stage to act. What were her feelings? I was not as much interested in those that related to the scene as I was in those experiences which somehow influenced her behavior on the stage. I was making little progress, when suddenly she blurted out that when she first started out as an actress, she was told she would never make it because of her looks and because she was too much of a lady to be an actress. As she continued, she revealed that it was her father who had initially opposed her becoming an actress, saying to her, "They're all tramps."

"That's why it was very hard here in the beginning, because he was visiting me at the time I started."

I said, "And every time you —"

"— would sit a certain way, or whatnot, he would say, 'That's not ladylike.' "

"And in what way did that affect your getting on the

stage? When you got up on the stage, you felt that you were making a tramp out of yourself?"

"The first scene I did for you,* he was here, too; and so when I was going to do my scene in my underwear, it just (*whew!*) blew his mind."

"Oh. In other words, he happened to be here the first time that you were doing a scene."

"Yes."

"What did he say? Never mind 'blowing his mind.' Let's hear what his words were."

"He said, 'You're not.' And I said, 'Yes.' 'If you're going to do your scene in your underwear and your slip, at least sit ladylike.' " [*Laughter*]

"Very important. And so when you got up on the stage, you were more concerned with —"

"— how to sit."

"— how to hold your legs rather than what to do with your character."

"Right. Because you said I was a blend between Blanche and Stella."

"I said what?"

"You said that you couldn't figure out whether I was Blanche or Stella. At that time I just wanted to leave."

"You're quite right. You're quite right."

"I didn't want to be there. Because I was so confused."

"No, you weren't confused. You were conditioned to a certain behavior."

Here was an instance of strong primary conditioning combined with the special circumstances of doing an important scene for the first time. All of the factors contributed to an original experience of tension that continued to affect expression on stage.

There are, of course, many pressures on the actor. One

---

* A scene of Blanche's in *A Streetcar Named Desire*.

pressure every actor is concerned with is remembering his lines. I can attest to my own reaction when, after many years of not performing, I was to do *The Godfather, Part II*. What troubled me most was not any concern about my acting, but, would I remember my lines? Would I hit the marks? This anxiety was something that I have always suffered from. When I was a young actor I had an excellent memory — I still do. I memorized lines very easily, and yet, whether in rehearsal or in performance, I would always go through attacks of anxiety. Before uttering the first line, I would repeat it again and again. Then, afraid I would forget it, I would whisper it over and over to myself until I entered the scene. Once I was there, my fear of forgetting disappeared. My concentration was always firmly on what I was doing. Yet for many actors this anxiety often can impede expressiveness.

In one instance, we were dealing with a very experienced actor. He seemed to me to possess much more power and emotional conviction than he had yet learned to deal with. He was rehearsing a scene from *The Night of the Iguana*. At the end of the scene, the actor usually describes to us both the problems that he set himself to deal with in the scene and those he experienced during the performance of the scene. This actor said that he had started to work on the scene before memorizing the lines. To his surprise, as he started rehearsal, the lines came on their own. The actor went on to say that the more he was dealing with what he was doing in the scene, the less of a problem he had with his lines.

"That's right," I told him. "If you're *doing* something, you know what you're doing. You know what the characters are talking about. If you won't say the precise line, you can say something else; therefore this fear is obliterated. But that's not what we need to be concerned with. What we need to be concerned with is that the lines should always seem to be not remembered. Either you remember the lines, or, if you don't, you know what the scene is and you can go on with it. Your partner will remember the lines. That's the least part of it. That is pure memory. That has nothing to do with acting. It has nothing to do with acting talent, it has nothing to do with what the actor does. Any human being has problems with memory, so that's not an acting problem. What is a problem is when the actor does deal with his own necessary concerns in the scene, and does not know how to make himself believe in it. Whereas, when the actor does believe in what he is doing, even if one word goes out, a line, a phrase, it's not that bad. The actor can say, 'I'm doing so many other things that are important, that fulfill me, that make me feel real, make me feel I have a right to say what I'm saying, I have a right to do what I'm doing,' and that's the basic thing that obliterates stage fright: concentration — concentration on things that you do that impel you, that give you something in return."

The more I investigated the problem of the relation between the actor's ability to create experience and his capacity to express that experience in vivid, dynamic terms, the more I became aware of and realized the nature of the actor's technical problems. I also discovered why actors seem to suffer anxieties of which neither the audience nor even the directors have any comprehension. It is not his understanding of the role that is at fault. If understanding were the primary requisite, the director, the critic, or the playwright would be the best actor.

The actor can, of course, coolly, and externally with the help of some technical training, carry out precisely the demands made upon him by the director, or, for that matter, by himself. The more complete involvement in and commitment to creating and sharing the life and experiences of his character the actor seeks, the more he will face the problems of dealing with and controlling his own human instrument. His instrument responds not only to the demands of the actor's will, but also to all those accumulated impulses, desires, conditioning, habits, and manners of behavior and expression. They are so automatic that the actor is not aware of them and is, therefore, unable to deal with them. The extent to which unconscious habits of thought, feeling, and behavior influence the actor during the actual process of acting still demands greater recognition and clarification.

It is important to differentiate between those actors who are inhibited from *feeling* emotion and those who experience very deeply and intensely, but have been brought up in an environment that did not encourage and develop their capacity to *express* this intensity. Under ordinary conditions of experience, they express themselves clearly and directly, but the stronger the experience, the less able they are to express it. Since there are no inhibitions standing in the way, there is no need to eliminate anything; it is only necessary to relax, and not to make use of the habitual forms of expression. Then the impulse will find and create new forms of expression that are more appropriate for the play than those the actor is accustomed to. As water seeks its own level, so it seems the nature of impulse to seek its own expression.

A lot of confusion has resulted from the misunderstanding of the work with the actor which I've described. Some charge that these issues are more properly within the sphere of the analyst, psychiatrist, or physician. The accusation has been made that this work really amounts to amateur analysis or "cheap" psychiatry. It is true that often the work leads to results unrelated to acting.

For example, after participating for a number of months in my classes, a young lady apologized for having to discontinue because she had become pregnant. My wife, Anna, was startled when the actress declared that I was directly responsible for her pregnancy. Noticing my wife's reaction, she hastened to explain. Doctors had told her she could not conceive. She had therefore decided to concentrate her energies on training to be an actress. When the doctor notified her of her pregnancy, he added that it was undoubtedly due to the relaxation that she had practiced in recent months.

The simple fact is that since I do deal with the total human being, the way in which he thinks, feels, emotes, behaves, and expresses himself, I cross areas that are dealt with in other contexts. But it should be emphasized that the intentions are quite different. The psychologist's purpose in helping his patient to relax is to eliminate mental and emotional difficulties and disturbances. In acting I am not concerned with eliminating either experiences or emotions. The intention is to help each individual to use, control, shape, and apply whatever he possesses to the task of acting. I am only concerned with pressures to the extent that they interfere with the execution of the tasks the actor sets for himself. I do not eliminate experience! I help each individual to become aware of the deepest sources of his experience and creativity and to learn to recreate them at will in the process of achieving an artistic result.

Throughout the ages, artists have suffered from various mental or emotional disturbances, from neurotic or even psychotic conditions. This at times may have added intensity and fullness of commitment to their work, as in the cases of Strindberg, van Gogh, or Artaud. However, the artist can take advantage of the inspiration that sometimes comes from the intensity of his disturbance, if the creative process can take place at any time, and need happen only once in order to produce the play, the novel, the painting. In acting, however, the creative process must occur at a definite time and place — that is, in a particular performance — and must be able to be repeated the next night. Therefore, I am only concerned with the conscious control of faculties which in other arts can and do work unconsciously or sporadically.

The basic aim of the actor's training is to give him as complete control as possible of those human faculties. This control is the foundation for the actor's creativity. Therefore, there is a basic difference, a totally different intention, between the direction of our work and the desired results and aims set by the psychotherapist. I have found that while individuals who practice Zen, Yoga, meditation, etc., are helped in their personal lives, such disciplines do not help them express themselves in their acting. Analysis of one kind or another helps an individual to become more aware of the functioning of his own nature. It may therefore be of some value in aiding him to understand and to practice the actor's craft. But it does not seem to be a necessary foundation for acting.

I have emphasized the above because many young teachers today who have been stimulated by the exercises and procedures of our training have mistaken these basic differences. They have actually embodied in their work various procedures which have no relation to professional acting and no direct connection with the problems that the actor encounters, and often distract attention from the concern with the basic artistic execution and theatrical problems of training. That is the primary concern.

To some, my training appears too inwardly directed. These critics, however, do not understand the fundamental nature of the actor's problem: the actor's ability to create organically and convincingly, mentally, physically, and emotionally, the given reality demanded by the character in the play; and to express this in the most vivid and dynamic way possible. While all art is for the creator a means of self-expression, it is only the extent to which it reveals what is experienced that it becomes art.

The Method is sometimes accused of making problems for the actor that never existed. Problems and difficulties have always existed; only their solutions and the discovery of methods to train the actor are modern.

The two areas of discovery that were of primary importance in my work at the Actors Studio and in my private classes were improvisation and affective memory. It is finally by using these techniques that the actor can *express* the appropriate emotions demanded of the character.

When the French director Michel Saint-Denis visited the Actors Studio and saw an improvisation, he was amazed. He seemed unaware of the fact that it was a basic element in Stanislavsky's procedures, and that we had already used improvisation in productions of the Group Theatre. There is, of course, no chapter on improvisation in Stanislavsky's work; yet the études that he describes were improvisations, used not only in the process of training, but in the actual process of production. Vakhtangov also used the études in an extraordinarily imaginative way.

Improvisation today seems to be considered either as a verbal exercise or a game that is supposed to stimulate the actor. A good deal of what is thought of as improvisation as an exercise in verbal invention is illustrated in some of the fine work of the Second City. Improvisation is also mistaken as a paraphrase of the author's words. Both of the approaches have little to do with the primary value of improvisation to the actor's training, by which I mean exercises related to an exploration of the actor's and the character's feelings.

Improvisation is best known in the theatre through the work of the commedia dell'arte actors who performed across Europe during the sixteenth, seventeenth, and eighteenth centuries. Besides their use of stock characters, established through masks and costuming, the troupes elevated improvisation to a creative and natural level. With only an outline of the play's plot posted on the edge of the stage wings, the commedia performer was expected to fill in the unwritten dialogue and actions with set speeches, often in colloquial language, and standard comic routines. This procedure produced a kind of naturalness and spontaneity that we associate with twentieth-century acting. Everything, even totally memorized speeches, assumed the impression of spontaneity, since no actor was exactly certain what his partner might say or do within the plotlines of the scenario. Commedia audiences sensed this new feeling, and ultimately this led to new ways of writing and staging plays. Certainly Shakespeare's and Molière's work is indebted to the influences of the commedia dell'arte actors: there is a freedom and freshness in their dialogue and in their use of colloquial speech.

Another great contribution of commedia dell'arte is in the development of realistic and believable characterizations on stage. A great deal of what was achieved by the commedia in this area was lost in succeeding periods and did not return to the stage until David Garrick, and later Edmund Kean, reinstated a naturalistic style.

Improvisation is essential if the actor is to develop the spontaneity necessary to create in each performance "the illusion of the first time."

Stanislavsky had correctly discovered that a major problem in acting derives from "anticipation." Everything the character is supposed to be aware of, what he will be asked, what he will be told, events that are supposed to surprise him, even his responses — these things the actor already knows. Regardless of the skill with which the actor may pretend not to know what will occur next on stage, his normal scenic activity is actuated by his memory — by his carefully prepared and memorized words and motions. This leads, even at its best, to an "indication" of what is supposed to be taking place.

The actor will say in character, "I don't understand," and will therefore pretend not to understand. But a real character who says, "I do not understand," is at that moment actively trying to find out what it is that is being said. Thus, the actor may suggest the *results,* while the character is actually concerned with thinking and discovering what it may possibly mean. An actor will ask, "Who are you?" and naturally wait for the reply. A real character, while perhaps waiting for an answer, is actively concerned with trying to discover who the person is. The face might look familiar or unfamiliar, he might confuse him with another individual, etc. When a character says, "I don't know where to go," he is usually concerned with where he might go. But an actor simply suggests that he doesn't know where to go without solving his dilemma.

A real character has a continuous aliveness, a continuous process of thought and of sensory and emotional response. This goes beyond the line of dialogue already supplied to him by the author. To stimulate a continuous flow of response and thought within the actor is the primary value of improvisation. Many actors believe that they truly think on the stage. They do not accept the premise that their thought is tied only to the memorized lines of dialogue. In the process of training or of rehearsal, I will often deliberately change objects, partners, or other details and demonstrate to them that they go right on doing and saying what they have prepared to do. Often an actor enters a scene and, because he already knows the outcome, is playing toward that end. By improvising, the actor finds a way to play the scene more logically and convincingly, not just from his own point of view, but also from the audience's.

In one session at the Actors Studio, I asked an actress to participate in a demonstration. I suggested that she choose a scene from a production in which she had actually appeared and that had presented some difficulty she would like to investigate.

She chose the scene in *The Three Sisters* where Masha confesses to her sisters that she's in love with the Colonel. She preceded the scene with an improvisation in which she appeared to open a door and enter a space that seemed somewhat confined. Then she knelt to pray. The relevance of this improvisation to the scene which was to follow was unclear. Then she finished the improvisation and exited. She then entered the set in which she was to connect the exercise to the play. She sat down on the sofa and picked up a pillow she lightly played with and seemed to embrace. Then she uttered the first line of the actual scene, "Sisters, I have something to confess. . . . I love that man." The reality with which she rendered the scene was startling in its naturalness and vividness. A mixture of tears and laughter spontaneously poured from her.

After she finished the scene, she explained what had just happened. She described her experience when she was first asked to accept the part and read the script. It was when she came to this scene in the play that she decided to do the role. She did not question her decision, nor was she aware of what motivated her. In the actual performance, however, she was never satisfied; nor were the critics and audience.

She had had difficulty in arriving at any personal experience that might be connected with this particular event. She could find no direct parallel in her own life. She remembered her original response when she first read the script and wondered what motivated her decision to play the role in the first place. She then realized something she had completely forgotten. When she was a child of six, she was forced to go to confession. She had little to confess, but the nun told her a story which moved her deeply. The Lord sent Saint Peter down to earth to bring back the most beautiful thing he could find. When Saint Peter returned, what he had brought back was unacceptable. He was sent back to find something more suitable, but again what he brought back was insufficient. Finally, he returned and extended a closed fist. As he opened his hand, there was a single tear. It was a tear of a child at confession, and the Lord accepted this as being the most beautiful thing Saint Peter could have brought back. This story had made a deep impression on her.

After hearing that story, she would try to force a tear at confession, with very little success. She would make up stories that might possibly bring some tearful response from her, but to no avail. She suffered because she had nothing to confess. This is what she had found in trying to analyze her own response to this scene. It was this memory that had unconsciously affected her decision to do the part. In the improvisation at the Actors Studio, the re-creation and acting out of this event made a perfect preparation for what otherwise had proven a difficult scene.

Improvisation leads not only to a process of thought and response, but also helps to discover the logical behavior of the character rather than encouraging the actor "merely to illustrate" the obvious meaning of the line. Actors are often confused by the fact that during scenes for which they were praised, they were aware of having thoughts unrelated to the play.

As I've said before, it does not matter so much what the actor thinks, but the fact that he is really thinking something that is real to him at that particular moment. The make-believe thinking that may coincide with the play is not real enough, though it may be sufficient to fool the audience. This is what we sometimes mean when we refer to acting as being only "indication."

The second major area of my work involves affective

Marilyn Monroe attending a class conducted by Lee Strasberg.

h Marilyn Monroe did of Lee Strasberg.

A sketch Marilyn Monroe did of herself while working on a scene for Lee Strasberg. Her caption reads, "I must concentrate."

Program of a production of
Liliom *Lee Strasberg directed at
the Westport Country Playhouse
with Tyrone Power and Annabella.*

Lee Strasberg and Isaac Stern at the Teatro Cologne in Argentina.

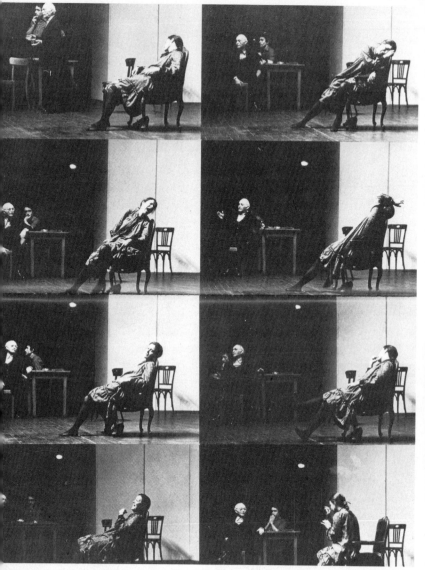

Lee Strasberg conducting an emotional-memory exercise in Germany. (Anna Strasberg is the actress.)

Lee Strasberg conducting a seminar in acting in Bochum, W. Germany.

Lee Strasberg in The Godfather, Part II *(1974)*

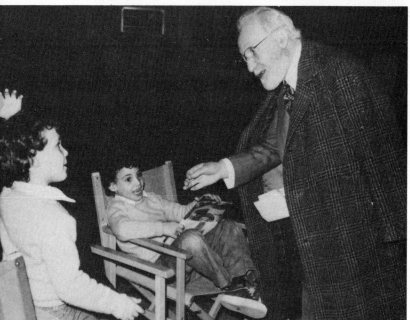

Lee Strasberg giving his sons David and Adam (seated) acting lessons on the set of The Cassandra Crossing, *in which the two boys appeared with their father.*

Lee Strasberg and his wife, Anna, in the garden of their home in California, 1976. (Photo courtesy of Betty Beaird)

The last photograph of Lee Strasberg, 1982. He is with his wife, Anna, and sons Adam and David on stage at the Actors Studio. (Photo courtesy of Ken Regan, Camera 5)

memory. As I discussed earlier, Boleslavsky divided affective memory into two categories: analytic memory, and the memory of feeling. Analytic memory is trained and developed by exercises involving imaginary objects; in our work we call this aspect of affective memory sense memory. The second category that Boleslavsky described was the memory of feeling, which we call emotional memory. My work at the Actors Studio and in my private classes revolved around emotional memory as part of the actor's training. (The generic term *affective memory* is often confused with the term *emotional memory*, but *emotional memory* pertains specifically to the more intense reactions of an emotional response. Stanislavsky and his circle often used the term *affective memory* to mean what we call *emotional memory*, the memory of feeling. In the following discussion, the terms are used to mean the same thing.)

The term *affective memory* was taken by Stanislavsky from a work by the French psychologist Theodule Ribot, *The Psychology of the Emotions*. This book was translated into Russian in the 1890s. (A copy of the book is in Stanislavsky's library.) Ribot noted in his chapter "The Memory of Feelings" that there had been numerous studies into the nature and the revivability of visual, auditory, tactile-motor, and verbal images, but that the question of the emotional memory remained nearly untouched. Our emotions and passions, like the perceptions of sight and hearing, can leave memories behind them. It is clear that these memories are provoked in life by some actual occurrence. His concern was whether or not these "emotions formerly experienced can be revived in the consciousness spontaneously or at will, independently of any actual occurrence which might provoke them."

Ribot in no way questioned the presence of emotional memories. He questioned only the extent to which these are capable of being revived at will. Many critics, unfortunately, have confused the existence of emotional memories with the difficulty that most people have in recalling them at will. It is precisely this problem of recall that was of major significance to Stanislavsky because of its application to all schools or styles of acting.

Ribot cited his own investigations in which he asked a variety of people to revive or recapture an emotional memory. In one of his studies, a young man of twenty made an effort to remember the feeling of ennui that he had experienced on his first day in the barracks. The young man shut his eyes and abstracted his thoughts. He first felt a slight shiver down his back, a feeling of something unpleasant that he would prefer not to have felt again. This uncomfortable feeling was connected with a vague sensation that did not firmly materialize. He then visualized the barrack yard where he used to walk; this image was replaced by that of a dormitory on the third floor. Then he saw himself seated at a window, looking through it, viewing the entire camp grounds. While the image soon disappeared, there remained a "vague idea of being seated at a window and then a feeling of oppression, weariness, rejection and a certain heaviness of the shoulders." Throughout, the feeling of ennui persisted.

Ribot noted that a characteristic peculiar to affective memory is the slowness with which it developed. Actually, I discovered that after sufficient exercise, the recall can be accomplished in one minute.

Ribot's discoveries obviously played a great role in Stanislavsky's growing awareness of the actor's unconscious procedures during the creative process. This presented a solution to a problem that had previously evaded comprehension: What happens when the actor is inspired, or what is the nature of the actor's inspiration?

Memory can be divided into three categories. First, there is mental memory, which can be easily controlled.

We try to remember where we were yesterday at this particular time, and most people will be able to do so. The second kind is physical memory, which teaches us how to control our muscles. During the process of learning, we are quite conscious of what we are doing, but after we have achieved it, it continues to be repeated automatically by memory. For example, at the age of five, my son David grandly announced that he was able to tie his shoelaces. It took five years to train his muscles to deal with that task. After a while, tying his shoelaces became habit; the memory functioned automatically. The third kind of memory is affective memory. It consists of two parts: sense memory and emotional memory.

Affective memory is the basic material for reliving on the stage, and therefore for the creation of a real experience on the stage. What the actor repeats in performance after performance is not just the words and movements he practiced in rehearsal, but the memory of emotion. He reaches this emotion through the memory of thought and sensation.

Psychologists disagree on the actual nature of emotion: What takes place psychologically? In what area is an emotion localized? How are emotions stimulated? How are they expressed? Many of these questions have not been answered sufficiently.

A startling study on the presence and the workings of affective memory (both sense memory and emotional memory) is the work of a Canadian brain surgeon, Dr. Wilder Penfield. In the course of surgically treating patients who suffered from epileptic seizures, he stumbled on the fact that electrical stimulation of certain areas of the brain occasionally produced a state in which the patient "relived" a previous experience. On first encountering these flashbacks in 1933, he was incredulous. A young mother told him she was suddenly aware of being in her kitchen, listening to the voice of her son playing in the yard. Each element of the original experience was reproduced: the neighborhood noises, the passing motor cars. Another patient relived an experience in a concert hall; each individual instrument was clearly defined.

In an effort to confirm his findings, Dr. Penfield was interested in further exploring the source of these sensations. He restimulated the same point thirty times. In each instance the subject "relived" the experience. Dr. Penfield called such responses "experiential." In real life, this process is stimulated by some conditioning factor that arouses it. For example, when someone tells you that he met a particular individual whom you have strong feelings toward, your heart starts pounding. You will find yourself reacting merely to the mention or suggestion of that person, even in his absence.

While mental or physical actions can be controlled at will, emotions cannot. You cannot tell yourself to be angry, to hate, to love, and so forth. Conversely, you cannot tell yourself to stop feeling any of those emotions once they are aroused. It is in this area that the startling methods of Boleslavsky and Madame Ouspenskaya have made the greatest contribution in acting.

The "inspiration" I had noted in my earlier years had occurred when a great actor worked unconsciously and was able to relive an overwhelming experience and express it in performance. I have spoken of Ben-Ami's inspiration in *John the Baptist*. But these actors were not always able to repeat the experience at will. Recreating or reliving an intense emotional experience at will was at the core of our work.

The actor trains himself to control "inspiration" through an "emotional-memory" exercise. To try to recapture or relive an experience, the actor needs to be first of all relaxed, so that there is no interference between the activity of the mind and the other areas that are being induced to respond. I discovered that the presence of mental or physical tension is often the result of anticipating the way in which the emotion should happen, and thus interferes with the spontaneous flow of sensation.

It is not necessary to go through the hours or days it took for an event to develop. The actor starts five minutes before the emotional event took place. The correct process of inducing a response is through the senses. He tries to remember where he was. Say he was in the yard. The actor cannot simply think in generalities. The yard is composed of many objects that he sees, hears, touches, and so forth, to which he assigns the word *yard*. Only by formulating the sensory concreteness of these objects can the emotions be stimulated. It is not sufficient to say, "It was hot." Rather, the actor must define precisely in what area he experienced the particular heat he remembers; the actor localizes the concentration in that area to create not just a memory but a reliving of that particular moment. The actor remembers what he had on: the sight, texture, or sensation of that material on the body. The actor tries to remember the event that caused the emotion, not in terms of the sequence of the story, but in terms of the various senses that surrounded it. If another individual was involved, he must be experienced in terms of sense memory as well.

As the actor comes closer to the moment of intense emotional reaction, the body will often exert a counter tension to stop it; nobody likes to relive intense experiences. When the actor arrives at the moment of high intensity, he must be able to stay with the sensory concentration; otherwise, the actor's will is out of control and he may be carried away by the emotional experience.

I have seen much fear on the part of many people when they first faced the problem of performing the emotional-memory exercise — fear of being carried away, as they put it, and of not being able to be pulled back, a fear which is perfectly natural because the human being is doing something that he is not accustomed to, and anything new is frightening. This is also a fear of losing control. The whole point of the emotional-memory exercise is to establish control over emotional expression. For this reason, the emotional memory work is preceded by extensive preparation work.

The fundamental work of the actor — the training of his internal skills — is preceded by the development of the actor's relaxation and concentration. Work in concentration leads to the development of the ability to use the senses not only with actual objects, but with imaginary objects. These procedures are described in detail in the next chapter.

Many critics of the Method object to the actor's use of affective memory, but these critics have failed to observe and appreciate the extent to which it is involved in the other arts. Affective memory is a decisive element in most artistic creation. The only difference is that in other art forms, the affective memory is created by the artist in the solitude of his own environment. In the performing arts, the artist must create in the presence of an audience at a particular time and place.

This link between affective memory and creativity has been a constant presence in poetry. In fact, the thrust of much of the Romantic movement in the early nineteenth century was an exploration and celebration of "the true voice of feelings." Both in their poetry and their critical writings, the English Romantics attempted to uncover the sensory foundations of their own creativity. Wordsworth wrote in "The Prelude":

> ... for I had an eye
> Which is my strongest workings, evermore
> Was looking for the shades of difference
> As they lie hid in all exterior forms,
> Near or remote, minute or vast, an eye
> Which from stone, a tree, a wither'd leaf,
> To the broad ocean and the azure heavens,
> Spangled with kindred multitudes of stars
> Could find no surface where its power might sleep.

In an analogous poem, Coleridge praises the bond between mental imagery and the creative spirit,

> O! What a life is the eye! what a strange
>   and inscrutable essence!
> Him that is utterly blind, nor glimpses
>   the fire that warms him;
> Him that never beheld the swelling breast
>   of his mother;
> Him that smiled in his gladness as a babe
>   that smiles in its slumber;
> Even for him it exists, it moves and stirs
>   in its prison;
> Lives with a separate life, and 'Is it
>   a Spirit?' he murmurs:
> 'Sure it has thoughts of its own, and to
>   see is only a language.'

Even Byron remarked that Wordsworth taught him how to look at a mountain using "the mind's eye" as well as objective reality.

Much of English Romantic poetry was a direct response to sensory experience: what the poets saw, what they heard, what they observed. Remembering the moment of creativity, when he composed the famous poem "The Daffodils," Wordsworth wrote,

For oft, when on my couch I lie
In vacant or in pensive mood,
They flash upon that inward eye . . .

Wordsworth's descriptions were not mere literary phrases, but the result of direct observation. When someone challenged his account of the enlarged appearance of sheep when seen through a screen of mist — "His sheep like Greenland bears" — it was corroborated that mist does actually exaggerate the proportion of an object. Even Wordsworth's sense of poetic sound, the breaking of ice, the humming of bees, the muttering of brooks, the twittering of birds — all these literary devices came from a remarkably attuned aural perception.

In our own century, the two greatest novelists, James Joyce and Marcel Proust, used affective memory in its most direct and graphic way. Virtually all of Proust's epic *Remembrance of Things Past* was an attempt to record the memory of experience within a sensory context. The taste of a cookie, the smell of a cigarette, the crease of a pajama bottom, the unusual position of his near-sleeping body — all these remembered sensations unleashed a flood of emotional memories that no pure intellect could.

Proust described the difficulty of recapturing the emotional past, a problem that almost everyone has experienced:

It is a labor in vain to attempt to recapture it: all the efforts of our intellect must prove futile. The past is hidden somewhere outside the realm, beyond the reach of intellect, in some material object (in the sensation which the material object will give us) which we do not suspect.

What follows from Proust's work is a clear and sensitive description of an affective memory and how it is evoked.

One day in the winter, as I came home, my mother, seeing that I was cold, offered me some tea, a thing I did not ordinarily take. I declined at first, and then, for no particular reason, changed my mind. She sent out for one of those short, plump little cakes called "petites madeleines," which look as though they had been molded in the fluted scallop of a pilgrim's shell. . . . I raised to my lips a spoonful of the tea in which I had soaked a morsel of the cake. No sooner had the warm liquid and the crumbs with it, touched my palate than a shudder ran through my whole body, and I stopped, intent upon the extraordinary changes that were taking place. . . .

And once I had recognised the taste of the crumb of madeleine soaked in her decoction of lime-flowers which my aunt used to give me (although I did not yet know and must long postpone the discovery of why this memory made me so happy) immediately the old grey house upon the street, where her room was, rose up like the scenery of a theatre to attach itself to the little pavillion, opening on to the garden, which had been built out behind it for my parents (the isolated panel which until that moment had been all that I could see); and with the house the town, from morning to night and all to attempt to make it reappear.

Not only does Proust's writing reveal a startling and detailed account of an affective memory, but his questioning and sharp analysis of its creative value point up the problem of the artist and his mode of inspiration and creativity.

And suddenly memory returns. . . . I was conscious that it was connected with the taste of the tea and cake, but that it infinitely transcended those savours, could not, indeed, be of the same nature as theirs. Whence did it come? What did it signify? How could I seize upon and define it?

Great painters are even more sensitive to sensory and emotional recall. The great abstract painter Wassily Kandinsky described an unusual capacity for retaining "real" visual imagery from his past. He recalled that even as a boy, he could "paint pictures from memory at home" that he had seen at exhibitions. He also recalled that in an examination in statistics, he was able to quote a whole page of statistics which appeared in his mind's eye. He could walk down a long street and later name every shop without making a single mistake because he seemed literally to see them again in his mind.

Entirely without consciousness I steadily absorbed impressions, sometimes, so intensely and incessantly that I felt as if my chest were cramped and my breathing difficult. I became so overtired and over-stuffed that I often thought with envy of clerks who were permitted and able to relax completely after a day's work.

As Kandinsky moved toward abstraction in his art, he noticed this ability had diminished.

At first I was horrified, but later I understood that the powers that made continuous observation possible were being channelled in another direction through my more highly developed ability to concentrate, and could accomplish other things now more necessary to me.

For Kandinsky, the next step was to relive images and experiences. He wrote:

Everything "dead" trembled. Not only the stars, moon, woods, flowers of which the poets sing, but also a cigarette butt lying in the ashtray, a patient white trouser button looking up from a puddle in the street, a submissive bit of bark that an ant drags through the high grass in its strong jaws to uncertain but important destinations, a page of a calendar toward which the conscious hand reaches to tear it forcibly from the warm companionship of the remaining block of pages — everything shows me its face, its innermost being, its secret soul, which is more often silent than heard.

Kandinsky's "relived" images were transformed into images in his paintings. Here is an example of the artist's ability to control, and, therefore, express his emotional experience.

Although T. S. Eliot was referring to the author's creativity in his essay *The Problem of* Hamlet, what he said there could also apply to the necessary relationship between artistic creativity and the practical techniques of affective memory we use in the Method:

The only way of expressing emotion in the form of art is by finding an "objective correlative"; in other words, a set of objects, a situation, a chain of events which shall be the formula of that *particular* emotion; such that when the external facts, which must terminate in sensory experience, are given, the emotion is immediately evoked.

The actor, therefore, uses the "objective correlative" of his own experiences to find a means of expressing the emotion his character needs to express on stage. Affective memory becomes the key to the actor's expression.

It should be noted that in all the performing arts except acting, the artist has an instrument outside of himself which he learns to control. The instrument that the musician works with — the piano, the violin — does not create mental or emotional responses of its own. Regardless of the emotional state of the performer, the instrument remains objectively calm and capable.

The actor's instrument, however, is himself; he works with the same emotional areas which he actually uses in real life. The self that the actor presents to the imaginary Juliet is the same as the self he uses in his most private and intimate experiences. The actor is both the artist and the instrument — in other words, the violinist and the violin. One can imagine what would happen if the violin or piano started to talk back to the performer, complaining that it did not like to be struck in a particular way, that it did not respond to certain notes, that it was embarrassed at being touched sensually by a performer. This interaction between the artist and his instrument is precisely what transpires when the actor performs. His body, his mind, his thoughts, his sensations, his emotions are separated from the objective intentions. The Method, therefore, is the procedure by which the actor can open control of his instrument, that is, the procedure by which the actor can use his affective memory to create a reality on stage.

THE FRUITS OF THE VOYAGE·
Procedures for the Actor's Training

―――――――――――

IN this section of the book I outline the steps and procedures of the actor's training that lead to his approach to a performance. This is not a "how-to" section. It is not intended to take the place of training under proper supervision, nor does it supply exercises that the actor can perform by himself.

It has been common to characterize acting as demanding belief, faith, and imagination. To believe, one must have something to believe in; to have faith, one must have something that encourages faith; to have imagination, one must be able to imagine something specific. The purpose of these acting exercises is to train the actor's sensitivity to respond as fully and as vividly to imaginary objects on stage as he is already capable of doing to real objects in life. He will, therefore, have the belief, faith, and imagination to create on the stage the "living through" that is demanded of the performer. This remains my own major emphasis.

Of course, the degree of living through, the choice of

the reality and the variety and intensity of the reality, varies from play to play depending on the demands of the playwright, the director, and the actor's own needs.

The sequence I intend to describe was not arrived at casually, but contains a basic logic derived from practice and experience. The sequence proceeds from the simple to the more complex; from objects that are in our immediate environment to objects that reside only in our memory; from objects that are external and clearly observable to objects that are internal and depend on our inner concentration to be recreated. We move from single objects of attention to combinations of a number of objects. Thus, the actor is prepared for the variety of problems that he will have to deal with in the scene and in the play. We then add words to the various actions that the actor has thus far created. If we come to the words too soon, which is the tendency of most training, the danger is that the reading of the line will become the major incentive of the actor; then, what the actor does will tend to remain only a pictorial illustration of the lines instead of relating to the behavior of the character.[*]

Everything we deal with in these exercises — relaxation, concentration, sense memory, emotional memory — was defined by Stanislavsky.

Every exercise and training session is begun with relaxation. The actor tries to discover and come in contact with those areas of the body which are tense. Tension is not

[*] The words prepare the actor to carry out the activities desired by the author. Yet, as early as the Group Theatre days, by the third day of rehearsal, the actors were already encouraged to get out of their chairs, and without any attention to staging, to walk around and permit the body to begin to function expressively, even though the script was still in their hands. They were not permitted to memorize the words of the play. At the same time, improvisation relating to the ·tor's and the character's feelings had already started.

emotional — worry, concern, or disturbance. A human being may experience these and still remain relaxed, and therefore able to deal with them. Tension is the presence of unnecessary or excess energy which inhibits the flow of thought or sensation to the required area. While ridding the body of tension completely is an impossibility, the actor must learn to control it so that it does not inhibit his willful commands to his body. Relaxation is equivalent to the tuning of the violin or piano. The musician may be giving all the right commands, but if the instrument is not properly tuned, the results will be unsatisfactory.

The very fact of performance creates tension for the actor. The scenic environment which requires memorization of lines, concentration, movement, and communication from the performer also creates unique external and internal pressures for him. The actor learns to relax not only to prepare for a performance, but to sustain the performance on stage. The actor deals with an instrument — himself — that continues to function on a subjective level in addition to obeying his objective commands. Proper control of his energy is a primary requirement.

It is easy to experience tension by trying a simple experiment. Try lifting something heavy, such as an edge of a piano or a heavy table. At the same time, try to solve a simple mental problem, such as multiplying 75 by 6 — an intellectual exercise that would normally involve little difficulty. You will discover that it is nearly impossible to do so while lifting the heavy object. The energy used in lifting makes it difficult for the brain to perform the mental task. Other areas of the body not actually involved in the lifting, such as the vocal cords, become unusually tense and therefore unable to function properly. If you attempt to recite a poem or sing a song or remember something, you will find it an insurmountable task. It is clear to see how tension can prevent the actor from controlling his expressive capabilities.

Neuromuscular tension makes it difficult for thoughts, sensations, and emotions to be transmitted and properly experienced. Often an actor is experiencing the emotion he is working for, but is unable to express it because of tension. I remember an actor who delivered a speech from a Shakespeare play which seemed external and mechanical. When he explained what he had attempted to do, it seemed impossible to believe him because we had seen none of it in his performance. When we made him relax properly, and then, while maintaining the relaxation, deliver the same speech, suddenly it was alive and convincing. This has been corroborated numerous times. The role tension and relaxation plays in human beings has recently begun to be recognized, but its importance for the actor is still insufficiently appreciated.

To achieve relaxation, the actor follows several simple steps. First, he finds a position in a chair that affords him some comfort and support for his body. Because the actor must be able to relax under many conditions, we prefer that he select a chair that is not particularly comfortable, but in which he could conceivably fall asleep, as he might on a bus, train, or airplane. Many people literally do not know what to do with their bodies. They simply stretch out in the chair with nothing more than a wish to relax. The actor must begin to become aware of what he can do with each area of his body to help himself fit into the chair so that he can achieve a state not simply of comfort, but of relaxation. One can be comfortable and relaxed, and uncomfortable but nonetheless relaxed. Comfort is nothing more than the habit we are accustomed to, and people tend to confuse this with relaxation.

Second, the actor begins to check each area of his body for the presence of tension. Usually he will sit statically and assume that thinking about relaxation accomplishes the result. We encourage the actor to check each part of his body by moving it and then directing the muscle or nerve to relax. Without the actual movement, the actor's mental command will lead nowhere. The muscular movement aims to connect the brain to the various parts of the body, since later it will have to obey that command on stage without any real motion. (It should be emphasized that the movements I describe, in and of themselves, accomplish nothing. Otherwise dancers and others who indulge in physical activity would be able to relax very easily, which is rarely the case.)

Physical relaxation is usually comparatively easy to accomplish. Mental relaxation turns out to be more difficult. In certain areas, physical tension can be eliminated only by lessening the mental tension. Quite unscientifically, but for purely practical application, we consider the mental areas of tension to reside in specific areas of the body. The first area is the blue veins at the temples. These are easily observed. Many people, when they feel tension, will instinctively massage that area of the brow and temple. On stage, the actor cannot rely on such massage. Everything must be controlled by his brain. All that is necessary to achieve relaxation is to try to release the energy, to feel the energy oozing out of this area. Though this may sound difficult, it is easy to do.

The second area of tension is at the bridge of the nose leading into the eyelids. This area becomes tense because it is active all the time, even when there is no particular need for the eyes to be observing. In fact, the eyelids periodically relax themselves by blinking. Only at moments of embarrassment or concern does this reflex become more obvious. Extreme and unnecessary tension builds up in the area of the eye to such an extent that many people, when they lie down to sleep and start to close their eyes, experience a sensation of falling, as if a weight were removed from the body. All one needs to do to achieve relaxation there is to permit the eyes to close a little bit, just as one does when going to sleep, to allow the energy to ooze out.

The third area of tension moves from the thick muscles at the sides of the nose that lead to the mouth and chin. This is the most trained area in every human being and therefore most subject to the buildup of tension. These muscles are directly and actively connected with the brain and the process of translating mental energy into verbal expression. Our verbal expression (speech) becomes so automatic that most of the time we are not aware of what we are thinking until we speak it. Tension often occurs in this area because it remains ready to respond, even when it is not necessary. To help eliminate this tension, we move the muscles in deliberately unhabitual ways, permitting the muscles and nerves to sag as when we are asleep or drunk.

The chin becomes particularly subject to tension. In checking tension in this area, it is sometimes impossible to move the individual's chin. He may open his mouth, but nonetheless the chin remains as tight as before. This area often remains resistant to manipulation intended to release facial tension. An area which often creates additional difficulty for the chin is the tongue. It performs quick, automatic actions that we are totally unaware of. Tension here is often difficult to deal with, but pushing the thumb under the chin somehow helps.

The fourth and central area of mental and physical tension is the back of the neck. All the muscles and nerves coming through the thick area of the shoulders and to the back of the neck and the cranium can create a severe bottleneck of tension that is very difficult to deal with. Many people complain of this tension. When a friend tries to aid them by massaging this area, they will often experience sharp pain. These thick muscles are strong enough to balance heavy weights, and yet the comparatively light touch of human fingers aiming to discern and ease the tension in them creates sharp pain. We try to help the actor by moving the neck around and from side to side, thus making contact with, and discovering, the areas that are tense. Once the individual has located the areas of tensions, the process of commanding them to relax turns out to be quite simple.

Another area of tension we have encountered and learned to understand over the last twenty years is the muscles and nerves in the upper and lower back. These muscles, according to some psychologists, retain the impression of strong emotional experiences, often of a dramatic nature. Until these muscles are relaxed, emotions cannot free themselves to be expressed.

During the relaxation exercises, the student will often encounter some emotion welling up from within himself which sometimes scares him and hinders his effort to relax. The actor's first impulse is to try to stop the emotion from happening or being physicalized. This usually takes place automatically, since it is part of the social conditioning that we all are subject to. We must try to permit this emotion to be expressed. This happens through a simple procedure: the actor makes an easily and evenly vibrated sound from his chest: "*Ahhhhhhhhhhhhhhhhhhhh*." The emotion is allowed expression through this sound. But he must remember to continue the movements toward relaxation, otherwise the sound will be a relief and not a release, and the habit of interference and nonexpression will be strengthened rather than eliminated. If the above procedure does not release the emotional experience but hampers the relaxation, the actor should then make a sharp, fully committed, and explosive sound from the chest:

"*Hah!*" This allows the expression of this stronger emotion.

Anyone trying this exercise by himself will usually discover that he really can't tell the difference between tension and relaxation. This can only be discovered with the help of a teacher who checks the actor. The actor becomes more and more able to differentiate between what he thinks is relaxation and true relaxation. Often, as his ability to relax develops, he himself will think he is more tense because he has become more aware of it.

None of the steps in the procedures described above will work if they are done mechanically. The actor must really be aware of his habitual positioning; must really check the various parts of his body for tension; must really move the parts of his body separately and at will; must really evaluate whether his efforts to relax are bringing the desired result; must really make contact between his brain and the parts of his body; must really commit fully to either of the sound-making procedures for promoting relaxation.

The role of tension, separate from mental stress, which has been well investigated, is often decisive enough to inhibit the carrying out of the actor's intentions in an acting procedure. The actor will claim that he is creating the desired reality, and yet none of it will be visible to the audience. In checking the actor's relaxation and eliminating the physical and mental tensions that are discovered, the belief of the actor is often verified. He is doing what he thinks he is doing, but the tension interferes with the creation of the reality and inhibits the reality from being expressed in other than the accustomed habits of non-expression.

Relaxation is only a prelude to the actor's central concern: the need for concentration. Everything the actor does is a two-sided action. Relaxation is connected with concentration.

One of the central requirements for the actor is the ability to repeat what he has done before and make it appear to be spontaneous. Something that has been precisely rehearsed must appear to be improvised. Contrary to the conventional understanding that the actor only performs one thing at a time, he must actually be concerned with a number of problems. He also must have a clear comprehension of where his major concern is at each moment, plus the order of significance of all the other objects that must be attended to at the same time. All of this depends on the actor's ability to control, divide, and adjust his concentration. The talent of the actor functions only to the extent that his concentration is trained. Concentration allows the actor to focus on the imaginary reality demanded by the play; therefore, concentration is the key to what has been loosely thought of as imagination.

The purpose of the concentration exercises is to train the actor to create and recreate any object, or group of objects, which combine into an event that stimulates the desired experience called for in performance. Thus, the actor is motivated into the necessary logical behavior of his character.

To concentrate, one must have an object of concentration; one cannot concentrate abstractly. The simple presence of an object will not induce concentration. If you look at a chair and try to concentrate, nothing will happen. If you start asking yourself simple questions — How wide is the chair? How tall is it? What is it made of? and so on — simple concentration will take place. But that, actually, is more a process of observation. The kind of concentration necessary for acting demands the ability to recreate something which is not there. It leads not only to the workings of the imagination, but also to the presence of that kind of belief or faith which has often been characterized as the essential element in acting.

I have already pointed out that in life, if we believe something is true, we behave as if it were literally true. The actor's task is to create that level of belief on stage, so that the actor is capable of experiencing the imaginary events and objects of the play with the full complement of those automatic physiological responses which accompany a real experience.

The training of concentration starts with the actor's ability to recreate objects which he encounters every day. He simply goes through each of his senses to check the extent to which they react and respond to that object. Once the actor learns how his senses function when that object is present, he then learns to recreate these reactions and responses when the object is not present. The route to concentration in these first exercises is through sense memory. The exercises involve imaginary objects.

The senses in life are unequally developed. Some people see better than they hear; some people taste more precisely than they smell. Therefore we must expect the same thing to be true in the exercises. By the process of exercising, we also strengthen the senses.

The first exercise deals with whatever the actor drinks for breakfast: coffee, tea, milk, orange juice. The actor first practices with the real object, trying to define for himself the elements which he refers to when he says, "This is real." He explores the weight and texture of the cup or glass, the sense of the liquid in the container, the temperature of the liquid as he experiences it through the container, etc. As the actor raises the cup to the lips, the weight changes and affects other areas of the arm. He explores the aroma, the temperature of the drink, and finally the taste. The actor then performs the exercise without the presence of the object.

Most individuals, when first asked to perform this exercise, complain that this is something that they do not think of when they drink. They are not able to perform the exercise except by simply muscularly imitating the way in which they handle the object. This, of course, is not what we settle for. Actually, it is not true that we do not think when we are doing such a simple task. It takes three or four years for a youngster to train his muscles sufficiently so that the cup reaches the lips without spilling. In observing children in their early years, it is interesting to see how the cup will reach almost every other area but the mouth. After this task is learned, however, it becomes habitual. The processes which have previously demanded great attention and awareness become automatic and the human being thinks that he loses awareness. However, a change in any one aspect of the experience — a sudden change in the temperature, for example — immediately arouses the individual's attention.

As I've said, the actor's tendency at the beginning of this exercise is to imitate his physical actions. Thus, when he starts the action of bringing the cup to his lips, he imitates the length of time in which it is ordinarily done. But if the actor is to recreate the sensory presence of the object, he will, in the process of bringing it to his lips, have to take a totally different time span to accomplish it. This time span depends on the extent to which his senses work. This is a logic followed in many other efforts of learning to do something. When someone reads lines, he reads very quickly, but in the process of memorizing them, he stops and starts, slows up and tries to remember, depending on the degree to which his memory actually functions. The ability to interrupt the automatic functioning of the nerves and muscles in order to create an object's presence for oneself, not simply to suggest its presence to an observer, is part of the process of creating reality rather than imitating it.

Interestingly enough, the very first exercise contains all the senses — touch, taste, sight, hearing, and smell —

rather than only one. But it remains the simplest exercise because the concentration is on only one object. One sense may work weakly and another may work with greater intensity. Only when the senses are stimulated by different objects, unrelated to each other, does the exercise become more complex and more difficult for the actor's concentration.

The second exercise in concentration is looking in the mirror — for the female, combing the hair and putting on makeup; and for the male, shaving. The actor actually practices these exercises while he's performing the real task at home. He then tries to repeat the reality without the presence of the objects. The emphasis is not on imitating the way in which he performs these common activities, but on the ability to recreate the objects that go into the performing of these tasks by means of sensory memory.

The logic behind choosing this as the second exercise is that it tells us something about the actor in addition to training the senses. We find that some people have no sense of themselves. Some are not able to see themselves in the mirror; others respond very subjectively and react in unusual ways to the sight of themselves. This exercise gives us an insight into the individual that we are dealing with and permits us to vary the sequence of the exercise accordingly. A subjective actor is not encouraged into a further subjectivity; on the other hand, the actor who has difficulty in making contact with himself can be stimulated into a greater awareness of his own presence.

We do not practice and repeat each exercise until it is fully accomplished. The actor should not be encouraged to challenge himself all the time. He will return to these exercises later on in his training, but in the meantime, it is necessary to check each of the senses rather than to stay with only one. The same logic is used in sports. No baseball pitcher starts training by pitching the ball to see how hard he can throw it. No football player starts immediately testing his ability to perform what is his specialty. On the contrary, they limber up, they exercise generally, they run, they do calisthenics, and then they easily start performing their specialties. Unfortunately, too many teachers push the actor to accomplish immediate results without permitting him to exercise his faculties, to get in shape.

If the actor has not responded well to the first two exercises, if he claims that he has no sensation whatever, I have found it valuable to use exercises where he can differentiate between muscular and sensory reality. The actor is asked to do something as simple as putting on and taking off shoes and stockings. This is a daily activity. We know the actor has the ability to perform this while he is talking or doing other things. Since he can practice it daily, it becomes a useful exercise to work on. Sometimes the actor is asked to work on the sensory taking off and putting on of underclothes because these objects are close to very sensitive areas in both men and women. These exercises help to stimulate the sensory response.

If the actor still has difficulty, I suggest working with three pieces of material of different texture, such as silk, fur, and some woolen material. The actor deals not with an entire object, but only with its texture. He practices with it by touching it, by floating it through the air to get the sense of its weight, by bringing it in contact with different parts of himself, face, neck, arm, and so on — parts of his body that would not ordinarily be involved in dealing with these objects. He usually discovers that his muscular behavior is the same with the three objects, but that the sensory experience is quite different. That helps him to distinguish between the muscular sequence, which is usually imitative and habitual, and the sensory response that we are trying to awaken.

If there is further difficulty, I often suggest that the student work with a real object in class, such as a hat or a pillow; he is to make it into a totally different object, like a child, a dog, or a doll. The presence of the literal object helps to focus the actor's concentration, and the presence of a literal sensation helps to stimulate or suggest the desired imaginary sensation. (This is an exercise suggested by Vakhtangov.)

If the actor continues to have difficulty, which happens rather rarely at this stage, we then deal with what we call a personal object. This is actually no different from any other object, but it must contain some element of personal significance. In order to arouse in the actor the search for some personal connection with an object, we describe the value in exaggerated terms: something that may have been given to him by somebody close to him who has died; somebody he loved and with whom he broke up; someone who killed himself. Obviously, very few people have objects with connections as strong as that, but it does give the actor a sense of the special nature of the type of object we are looking for. In trying to recreate the object, the actor deals with it no differently than he would any other object. He does not make an effort to capture the special significance or the emotional response connected with it. However, because the object does have a built-in personal experience, it will invariably trigger a response — maybe not the first time, but often by the second or third time.

After the second exercise (looking in the mirror), we switch to an exercise where no muscular movement is involved. The actor works on sunshine. He is not permitted to imitate the position or the manner which he really assumes while in the sun; for example, he's not permitted to stretch out or lie on the ground. Instead, he sits in a chair, he imagines the sun where it was at the time he practiced the exercise with the real sun, and he tries to recreate what he felt at that time in his body. In addition, he is encouraged to move the particular area of his body that he is concentrating on toward the sun. The movement acts as a stimulus for that area of the body to respond to the command of the brain. At the same time, he relaxes the other areas of his body, which, at that moment, are not involved in the concentration. In this way he prepares himself to be able to create the sensation of sunshine. Yet, by exercising control over his body, he is able to do things not only for the sake of relaxation; he is training himself to exercise a control that might be demanded by the action of a play.

The exercises then continue, testing not only the presence, but the intensity of sense memory. We check the intensity of the actor's response through exercises involving sharp pain. Here, for the first time, the actor is not dealing with an object he can practice with; rather, he is dealing with the memory of a sensation. The pain the actor chooses to work on should not be an overall sensation, but should reside in one area, so that the concentration knows exactly where to go.

The actor's initial reaction to the sensation should have been intense. If he is capable of recreating it, we expect to see the same intensity of reaction. Many actors are initially startled by the intensity of their imagined reality. In the back of their minds they always tend to think of imaginary reality as nonexistent and created by some image of reality. But they now become aware of the real strength of imagination. The recreated pain occurs to an extent they have never themselves believed possible. Now, for the first time, they realize that acting is not just make-believe; the imagination of the actor cannot only conceive but recreate an experience, which convinces the actor of his own presence and reality and thus forces him to have faith in what he is doing.

In other exercises, we continue to explore the intensity of sense memory. In the exercise involving sharp taste, we ask the actor to work with a real object, such as a lemon or some vinegar. By practicing at home with the actual object, he is able to confirm to what extent the sense memory is working. He goes on to deal with a sharp smell, a sharp noise, etc.

The actor then proceeds to an exercise involving overall sensations. An overall sensation is not experienced locally, but with the entire body. We usually start with exercises like a bath, then a shower, then a steambath or sauna (or, for people who haven't experienced the latter, a cold wind). For many people a special sensation is walking or standing in the rain. These exercises seem to play a major role in the full awakening of the actor's response.

The value of the overall-sensation exercise is twofold. First of all, it develops the senses and the kind of sensations that are connected with them. Second, I discovered that it helps to unblock areas of the individual that may be locked or inhibited. It is not necessary to know where the block is or even that it exists. We've discovered that almost all human beings have areas of inhibitions, self-consciousness, and embarrassment which make it difficult for them to express as fully on stage as they experience in private.

In performing the overall-sensation exercise, most actors have a problem in recreating the experience fully. They might stand in the shower and think; or if they're in the bath, they simply lie there and try to summon up the picture and concept of the bath. Under those conditions, the actor experiences inner concentration and a memory of the real experience; he does not arrive at the sensation he is working for. For the experience to be recreated, it has to be thought of not as one unit of experience; rather, each area of the body must try to recreate the specific sensation that it has in response to, for instance, the water.

A shower is experienced separately and differently by different parts of the body. Each area of the body is capable of generating independent responses. If you go over to a woman you do not know and touch her on the shoulder, she will turn around and say, "Yes?" If you go over to her and touch her on the behind, she is going to react quite differently. It is the same body and the same person, but the reactions are different.

Every area of the body, while it's part of the totality, is capable of independent reaction in the human being and, therefore, in the overall-sensation exercise. Often an actor comes in contact with an area that may be blocked, of which he has not even been aware. This is nothing to be worried about. It only suggests that something is being withheld, and anything withheld in one area blocks all other areas. Often without any need to analyze, without any need to theorize, the actor induces sensation in that area and thus overcomes certain unconscious inhibitions or locked-up sensations. Therefore, in this exercise, we often encounter strong emotions.

As we unblock them, a lot of sensations begin to pour through and begin to lead toward a fullness and vividness of expression. All actors desire this, but for most it is difficult to achieve, except on a somewhat external level.

But the overall sensations which I have described often lead to a more personal sense of exhibition. The key may perhaps reside in the fact that there is the element of nakedness involved in a shower, etc. For most people, this creates strong inhibiting reactions. At the end of the exercise, I will usually check the actor's own belief in what he is recreating. I say, "All right, okay, now stand up slowly, maintain the exercise, keep the exercise going; turn and look at me." Invariably the people will turn around and they cannot look at me, even though the exercise has been done fully clothed. They laugh, they blush, they respond in an embarrassed way without necessarily being able to tell me why. On questioning, they will admit that it is because they feel naked. It's a demonstration again of the extent to which the imagination can go. After all, they know that they are dressed; yet the strength of the imaginary reality that they have created is of the same intensity as if it were literally true.

In some instances the reaction is different. When they turn around and look at me, not too much happens. They seem a little bit self-conscious, but somehow they don't mind being watched. Some actors seem to love it. They love to have the feeling of nakedness in front of people because of a confined desire for what we call "love," not in the literal sense, but in the sense of reaching out, of wanting to be part of something. It's not simply sexual: they want to make contact with people and they have great difficulty doing that. Therefore they are shy. When I draw their attention to this desire to make contact and suggest that somehow they seem to like the exposure provided by the exercise, they will respond, "Oh, yes." It's as if something were released in them. It seems to permit the expression of a sensation which in many individuals is strong, has usually been locked up, and can now be shared.

Part of the therapeutic value of art generally, especially of the acting profession, resides in the ability to share experiences and emotions that are otherwise locked and blocked, incapable of being expressed, except under artistic and controlled conditions. This should not be confused with exhibitionism.

By now, the actor has had an opportunity to begin to exercise his basic sensory equipment, including the kinetic ones. He can continue for the rest of his life dealing with many diverse objects related to the functioning of the senses. The actor on the stage never has only *one* problem to deal with. He must always be aware of and able to deal with many problems at the same time.

Some critics of the Method question whether the actor can really accomplish a true and complete living-through of a part. They ask how it is possible for him to be the character and believe what he is doing, and to attend to all the other demands of the play — to remember the lines, follow the commands of the director, etc. — *at the same time*. This is precisely what the actor is capable of doing, and this is what leads to the second stage of the actor's work, dealing with more than one exercise at the same time.

By this time in the work, the actor has practiced creating the overall sensation described above. But to that we now add an object. This is where I ordinarily use the personal object. Any other could be used, but because the personal object evokes a stronger response, it is particularly useful at this point. The actor creates the overall sensation and maintains that sensation; at the same time, he creates an imaginary personal object. At this point the actor is permitted to make the sounds (*"Ahhhh"* or *"Hah!"*), long or short, either even and easy or sharp and explosive, depending on the degree of the response that seeks expression.

We now add deliberate vocal action, usually a song which can be sung or hummed with or without words. The words can be used separately from the melody. The purpose is not to permit the sound to be performed in the habitual rhythm and tonality, but to permit it to be colored by the reality that the actor is creating. The actor's tendency is to sing the song the way it is supposed to be done, even if he is not consciously aware of doing so. What we try to achieve at this point is the opposite. This begins to prepare the actor to deal with a problem that becomes more important in actual production.

Let us assume the actor is playing the part of Hamlet in a production directed in a new and original interpretation. The director insists that while Hamlet performs the soliloquy "To be or not to be," he is drunk and laughing hysterically as if it were all a joke. The actor is forced to struggle with his unconscious tendency to deliver the speech in the low, intense, thoughtful, or spiritual tone commonly associated with it. Though he may be able to create the drunkenness and the laughter, every time he has to speak, "the muscle of the tongue" (to use Stanislavsky's phrase) would drag him back to the conventional delivery. What we begin to prepare the actor for at this early stage of his training is to fight against conventional verbal patterns. The effort now is to train the actor to control his involuntary habits of delivery and to permit the words to take on whatever meaning may derive from the actor's experience or behavior. Thus, the actor is capable of results which he himself might not anticipate nor agree with.

The exercises continue to become further complicated when additional problems are added. In addition to the overall-sensation, personal-object, and sound exercises, the actor may be asked to create physical activities which are part of a daily occurrence, such as getting dressed, washing the face, brushing the teeth, combing the hair, making breakfast, and so on. Attention must be paid to the logical sequence of these activities. The actor continues to deal with the demands of his own creativity and at the same time maintains a necessary physical logic. Of course, all these additional elements of attention demand full sensory reality and not simply muscular imitation.

At this point in the training we will usually add a monologue such as the one from *Hamlet* already mentioned. The actor does not act this monologue with the meaning that it may have in the immediate context of the play; rather he permits it to be affected by whatever sensations he is working on. Thus, the monologue may be delivered in a sauna by someone who is responding to some personal object, who at the same time is sleepy, getting up, etc. The words take on utterly new meanings and dimensions that might be demanded by a particular director's interpretation.

After the actor has already performed this exercise fully, we test his responsiveness to direction. We may ask him, while he continues to maintain what he has done, to add a completely new adjustment (such as pain), and to go through the same sequence again. He must make sure that the words will be permitted to adjust to this additional element. By now, we are beginning to deal not only with the problems of creating the reality, but also with the problem of expressing that reality in diverse ways. This prepares the actor for all kinds of demands that may be made upon him in rehearsal and in production. He often may not agree with these demands, but nonetheless, he must be capable of executing them perfectly.

It is at this point that I begin to encourage the actor to go beyond his everyday, casual behavior and permit a fullness and vividness of expression which he rarely indulges in except in what I call the private moment.

Having realized that the actor's behavior on the stage is often limited by the habits of expression which he has developed in life, I searched for other possibilities that would help to strengthen the actor's expressiveness. One set of exercises was suggested by a well-known phrase of Stanislavsky's about the actor's capacity to establish for himself the necessary privacy on the stage in order to stimulate his concentration to work — the actor's need to be "private in public." I had come across this phrase often and had not seen any significance beyond that of the need to concentrate. Rereading it on one occasion, however, it occurred to me that people usually possess behavior which they perform in private that they do not indulge in publicly. In the midfifties I began to develop the private-moment exercise.*

Many people, especially women, have difficulty in carrying a tune. They never sing, except in private, and they stop as soon as anyone, no matter how close that person may be, interrupts the privacy. When asked what they were doing, they will usually answer, "Nothing at all." That is an example of a simple, but very true, private moment. People talk to themselves in private; they talk to others in private. They are not crazy, but they have things within them that they have not been able to express, and they do so in private. Many people dance and behave in vivid ways, but only in private.

Privacy is not to be confused with being alone. One can be alone and not private. In fact, one can be private even when one is not alone. But under those conditions the expressiveness would be inhibited and therefore it has no value for us as an exercise. A private moment is not characterized by the nature of what takes place, but by the particular sense of privacy which it possesses for the actor who expresses it. Thus, to the observer, the private moment in itself often does not seem to be private at all. It is not the deed itself which is private, it is its significance to the individual that makes it private. Therefore, the ability to perform a private moment in public — when the actor knows full well that he is being observed — becomes a valuable training device.

---

* The term unfortunately has often been misunderstood because the very word *private* has, for some people, suggestive connotations. Once a psychiatrist called my office to ask if it might be possible for him to observe "one of those private, obscene moments." *Private* suggested to him something reprehensible or sexual. While there certainly are incidents and examples of this in private behavior, the exercise itself is not like that at all.

The procedure of creating the private moment is very simple. The actor chooses a certain behavior in his life which he does only in private, and at no other time. He feels so special about this behavior that he stops it if he is interrupted by the appearance of another person. If he is questioned about it, he will deny that anything unusual has been taking place. As in other exercises, when the actor practices the private moment, he does not try to repeat or imitate it. Once he aims at a preconceived result through repetition or imitation, his awareness of an audience only intensifies. Part of the function of the private moment is to permit the actor to lessen this concern with the audience and to give himself fully and unself-consciously to the experience that he is creating.

The actor starts by creating the place, the environment, the room in which the private behavior usually occurs. He then adds the conditions that usually motivate this behavior; for instance, he is forced to question whether he should continue as an actor, or, as a result of some insult, he worries about his appearance. The actor does not now imitate what he has previously thought or done. He now truly tries to perform the exercise by dealing with the original motivation. If he has difficulty, he goes back to creating the place where the behavior took place. If he doesn't feel motivated to behave as he had originally, he doesn't. If he were private, he would. Therefore, obviously, he is not private enough. Thus he keeps strengthening his attention through concentration on the place and its element of privacy. His concentration and degree of involvement must deepen. He thus strengthens his facility to be private in public.

My development of this exercise has led to unexpected discoveries. I had always thought that regardless of any degree of reality, soliloquies were only a theatrical device, which, from a technical point of view, they obviously are.

It was my shock and surprise to discover how much people soliloquized in real life; how much they engaged in imaginary confrontation with other people with a fullness and vividness which they could not summon in public under the actual conditions. Therefore, in addition to whatever value this exercise possesses for the actor, it is of enormous benefit in helping him to play precise scenes involving soliloquies — not only in Shakespeare and the classics, but also in Chekhov, where there are many moments which are the equivalent of soliloquies. For example, in *Uncle Vanya*, Sonya returns to the room after Astrov has left. She describes not only her exhilaration, but also her concern about her looks and about what people feel about her.

The private-moment exercise proves equally beneficial in dealing with operatic moments, which are actually nothing more than soliloquies — for example, the famous scene in *Der Rosenkavalier* when the Countess observes herself in the mirror and ruminates on the ravages of time; or the last scene in *La Traviata* where Violetta examines herself in the mirror and expresses the fullness of her despair, hopelessness, and desires. These are usually thought of as theatrical devices. Actually, they are true revelations of human events that take place in private. The private moment has taught us that people's behavior in private is not only more expressive and more vivid, but more dramatic than one might ever imagine.

I do not stop with the private moment. Rather, the private moment becomes a starting point for the other exercises that the actor has already practiced. The actor creates the private moment and maintains it as he adds other elements unrelated to it: the overall sensation, a personal object, daily activities, a monologue, a song, and so on. I have the actor do this, however, only after he is capable of creating the private moment with sufficient conviction and commitment. This exercise is one that the actor does until he has accomplished it. The exercise itself usually lasts about an hour, which means that the actor is capable of sustaining it for what would be the length of a long act on the stage, or the span of time typically demanded on a movie set.

I usually add at this time the animal exercise. This helps the actor approach a part by recognizing the difference between himself and the character. This exercise trains the actor by forcing him to deal with the character's behavior rather than relying on his own feelings. Sometimes with individuals who have a strong subjective streak, and whose emotions lead to static behavior, we use this at an earlier stage to get them away from their own subjective feelings and to strengthen their mental and physical attributes.

The specific value of the animal exercise is that it leads toward physical characterization. The exercise does not at the beginning demand any sensory experience except that of pure observation. It does not demand any inner concentration on oneself. The actor observes a particular animal in order to discover and register exactly how the animal moves. He then tries objectively to imitate those movements. He soon perceives that this imitation demands a totally different kind of energy in various parts of the body than that which he himself possesses. The human being is able to move areas which the animal cannot move. To imitate the paw, for example, the actor simply moves his arm; the animal, however, has no independent energy in that area. It cannot even hold its paws up and stand in the way that a human being does so easily in imitating it.

First, the actor notices the purely physical differences between himself and the animal, then he creates these differences by the control of his physical energies. There is no emotion, there is no sensation to begin with. Therefore, the actor practices objective observation and begins to be able to control, define, and command the areas within himself to do what the animal does. He learns to repeat with his own body the animal's physical energy, to build toward a sensation of the physical life of the animal — the strength and power of the lion, the sleepiness of the cat, the strange way the monkey observes what the human being is doing, and so on. Thus, the actor learns to practice and imitate the animal, physically, and with a sensory attribute contained within the physical activity. At this point, the actor stands the animal up, still maintaining the energies that the animal has. Even if the actor has never actually observed the animal stand up, he tries to create how it would be done. The actor uses the sound of the animal and often adds words spoken with the animal sound. This process continues until we make a human being with animal characteristics. Therefore, it becomes a character. When you take the chimpanzee, for instance, and you stand it up and make a character out of it, it's not a chimpanzee anymore. It becomes a character speaking in a human voice with human intonations, but having the characteristics of the animal. This helps the actor to create a particular type of human being — a character — that is separate from himself. The exercise leads to physical characterization in a performance.

Some actors dread the animal exercise. It seems as if they are almost afraid of becoming animals. This turns out to be nothing more than a struggle with their own habitual behavior. The demand of performing the animal behavior, of making the body do things which it is not accustomed to doing, creates a struggle with the actor's habits, which literally leads to a fear of the reaction.

An exercise that the actor is introduced to very early in his training and is encouraged to use easily without demanding immediate and intense results is the emotional-memory exercise. It is central to many of the greatest moments in performance. In the sequence of the work, if

I have not done so before, I now check it to make sure it is properly done.

In the emotional-memory exercise, the actor is asked to recreate an experience from the past that affected him strongly. The experience should have happened at least seven years prior to the time that the exercise is attempted. I ask the student to pick the strongest thing that ever happened to him, whether it aroused anger, fear, or excitement. The student tries to recreate the sensations and emotions of the situation in full sensory terms. He must recreate the circumstances which led up to the experience: where he was, who he was with, what he was wearing, what he was doing, and so forth. I tell the actor, "Do not pick a recent experience; not that the recent thing won't work. But the older the experience is, the better it is. If it works, it's going to last for the rest of your life. Whereas, something recent might work now and two years from now it won't. The fact that something has already worked, has existed for a long time and then is recaptured, means it is there for all time."

The actor begins the exercise. He does not tell me the story. He is not to worry about feelings or emotions, only the sensory objects — what he sees, hears, touches, tastes, smells, and what he is experiencing kinetically. The student shouldn't tell me, "I'm in a room." What he must do is describe the sensations as he tries by sense memory to recapture them, just as though he were doing an exercise in concentration.

Some acting teachers misuse this exercise. They want to know the stories. I don't want to know. The less the actor tells me, the better. I only talk to the student if I feel he's having some difficulty or if I want to check where his concentration is.

Here is an example of the procedure in the emotional-memory exercise that was taped at a session I conducted in one of my classes. It begins with the actress saying, "It's cold." We then go on to see if the actress is locating that sensation in different parts of the body — the hairline, etc. The actress then says that she feels a certain kind of cold in certain places.

"Well," I say to her, "take each place separately and try to see if you can remember the kind of cold that existed there. And see if, with the memory, you will be able to recapture some of that cold. And don't worry if it doesn't happen; just make the effort. Don't worry if you cannot swim. You simply keep moving your arms; you won't drown."

As the exercise proceeds, I ask the actress to remember what she was wearing, the material, etc., in an effort to recreate more details. The actress remembers that the material felt cold on her hands.

The exercise then continues as the actress recreates more of the details: the crinkly sound of the ground; later a dusty smell in the air; still later a voice, "shallow, like an echo." As the sound of the voice becomes stronger for the actress, she begins to sob.

"Wait a minute! Wait a minute, wait a minute!" she wails as the emotion breaks through.

In recreating the details of the original emotional memory, the actress recreated the original emotion. (Remember that we did not ask for the story of the original memory — just the details that would help recreate it.) It doesn't matter that the actress has lost words to describe what she's feeling: the playwright will give the actress words on stage. But the actress has tapped into an emotion she can recreate at will.

At this point, I stop the exercise:

"Right. Now, have we already touched the high point of the scene? We've touched it. Okay, that's enough then.

That's enough. Look at me. Open your eyes. You want a handkerchief."

I always forget that for these exercises we need Kleenex.

What the actress experienced was the full re-creation of an intense emotional experience. In being able to recreate it and express it, the actress develops the ability to control the expression of her emotions on stage.

In his final period, Stanislavsky made an effort in his research to stimulate the actor's reality and emotion by simple and unforced methods. Unfortunately, Stanislavsky's correct statement that emotion cannot be directly forced has led to the erroneous conclusion that it cannot, therefore, be stimulated. Stanislavsky never gave up the demand that the actor should be capable of living through a part. However, because of the difficulties he encountered, he hoped to stimulate the actor, who was already trained to the emotional response, by means of psychophysical actions.

I have found no difficulty in using the emotional-memory exercise and have developed specific procedures for its use. I demonstrated the way it can be used at the international seminars I gave in Paris, Argentina, and Germany. On every occasion, the observers were startled by the quickness and ease with which it was performed, and at the ease with which the actor could change from one emotion to another. It seemed for the first time to make the actor capable of satisfying those demands for inner precision and definiteness which Gordon Craig was asking for when he demanded that the actor be a "Super ('Über') Marionette." Through the proper use of emotional memory, the actor possesses a skill and flexibility on the stage.

An exercise of great value in achieving that connection between impulse and expression, which leads to full and intense expressiveness, is the song-and-dance exercise. I discovered this exercise in the midfifties. In addition to my work as a director and at the Actors Studio, I had private classes in a studio at Carnegie Hall. Among those who joined those classes were some singers and dancers who also desired to learn how to act. The musical play had come into its own in the forties with *Oklahoma!* by Richard Rodgers and Oscar Hammerstein II. (It had been preceded some time before by the Group Theatre's production of *Johnny Johnson,* written by Paul Green with music by Kurt Weill.) Now singers and dancers desired to prepare themselves for new dramatic tasks demanded by musicals like *West Side Story* and *Fiddler on the Roof.*

Since both singers and dancers necessarily have to follow a definite rhythmic and physical pattern that might confine them as actors, I tried to devise some simple exercises that would help them break their verbal and movement patterns. For example, the dancer must adhere to the prescribed dance form, but the actor must be able to move within that form as the character and situation demand. In order to help the actor achieve this, I developed the song-and-dance exercise.

This is an exercise in which the actor is asked to do something that is obviously easy to do, but goes against the grain of his training and habit. First I ask the actor just to stand on the stage in front of us, to look at the people — not to act, just to stand relaxed. The first few times I tried this, I discovered that the actors immediately fell into a pose. They set their feet wider apart than necessary to give themselves a feeling of security. I called that the "Atlas stance." This suggested to me that the actor was already carrying all the worries of the world and not just his own. When I questioned the actors, they usually agreed that they were unconsciously anticipating difficulty. Then the actor usually changed to a different position, bringing his feet closer together. That too is not a normal, relaxed attitude. I called that the "military stance." It means: "I will do what you want me to, not what I want to do. I have no will of my own, I am just obeying you."

I say to the actor: "No, that's not it either. I don't want it to be 'military' and I don't want you to be 'Atlas.' I just want you to be yourself, to hold yourself up, which means that you stand straight and at ease, that you find without working too hard, without making any undue effort, what might be called your center, and that your legs simply come out easily from your body to maintain you, just to hold you without any unnecessary effort — not setting yourself to anticipate difficulty, not settling yourself on a broad base as in football so that whoever comes at you won't bowl you over."

In a second exercise, I have the actor choose any song that he wants and try to sing it differently than the way he is accustomed to doing. Instead of singing the song continuously, I ask him just for the sake of the exercise to separate each syllable of each word; to give each syllable equal value with good vibrated tone that should nonetheless retain the melody. The reason for this is to show that he can, as a pure exercise of will, sing the song in an unaccustomed way. Let's say the actor takes a song as simple as "Happy Birthday." Instead of singing it in his usual way, he starts by singing,

"Hap — py — birth — day . . ."

"No," I say, "Not quite that way, just take each syllable and give it a full value — 'Haaaaaaaaaaaaaaaaap.' Take your time: check to see without moving that you are relaxed; check with the brain. Take new breath into the lungs, then the same thing with 'py': 'pyyyyyyyyyyyyyyyyyyyyyyyyy.' Commit yourself, make the sound. Then: 'Birrrrrrrrrrrrrrrrrrrrth.' Each sound is equal for no special reason, just to show that the sequence of the melody does not tire you, but that you have control of it."

What happens is that the actor will start — "Haaaaaaaaaaaaaaap-py" — and continue until the breath gives out. He can't stop himself. I say, "No, no. First of all, you are not supposed to move. Make each sound fully and separately; take a good breath in between so that you show you were in control of your own faculties."

Then the actor realizes and accepts the fact that while he might not have been aware of it, he was, nonetheless, subservient to the pull of habit. The exercise of the actor's will can help him accomplish the task. That realization is good for the actor.

I discovered in leading this exercise at first that strange things — seemingly unrelated to the exercise — began to happen. The actor would stand there ready to start; I would say, "Start." Some people would start crying, some people would start laughing. I could not understand why. I had not asked them to act. There was nothing special to do here except the simple exercise of will. When this behavior did not take place, however, and the actor would start to do the exercise, I found that he would make involuntary nervous movements — for example, the fingers on his hand would suddenly move. There was nothing especially wrong with that, but I would tell the actor, "Your fingers are moving." He would say, "No." I would say, "You don't know your fingers are moving?" He would say, "No." This was happening without his awareness.

This led me to the simple realization that I had unconsciously discovered something of additional value: the actor's basic attitude when he faces the public. No matter what the actor is prepared to do on the stage, he is more concerned with the audience than he is with what he should be doing. In this particular exercise, I discovered that the actor did not have any imaginary life to hide behind; there was nothing to deflect his attention from the audience. His stance captured all the locked-up concern about the audience. This was the first time I was aware that the actor could be concerned about the audience even when he was not called upon to act. The mere attitude of standing before the public would start many things going in the actor, even when he was called upon to perform a seemingly simple task.

There had to be a way for the actor to control his will in this situation. I told the actor to be aware of what was happening to him. Often he would be trembling even though I couldn't see it. At times I saw the presence of some emotion that was difficult to define and that the actor seemed to be unaware of. I then demanded that he find out what that emotion was. I told him that if he had difficulty, he should ask himself questions: Is it fear? Is it embarrassment? Is it anger? Is it frustration? Is it love? (not in the literal sense, but in the Freudian sense: not to embrace, but to be embraced by). The actor was then told to let that emotion simply go into the sound of the song.

Next I added a simple exercise as a pendant to the "song" exercise. The actor again stands at ease; he then commands himself to move without knowing in advance what he is going to do. Most actors, especially the dancers, would invariably start making dance movements. They were unconsciously relying on their habits and had difficulty in committing themselves to something other than what they were accustomed to doing. I then encouraged the actor to command himself to move. The actor starts with a bending movement — bending the body toward the floor and then back. He then throws himself into some kind of physical gesture without having any idea in advance of what it is going to be. I then ask him to repeat whatever gesture he made. The time interval involved in the repetition thus created a rhythm. The actor is supposed to repeat both the movement and the rhythm to prove that he can be both spontaneous, as the actor must be on stage, and at the same time able to repeat what he had spontaneously arrived at.

Dancers seem to have a special problem with sound. Often the strengthening of the body muscles seems to tense and tighten the vocal cords. I would ask an actor while he is making the movements of the exercise just described to use the sounds of the song. The sound is to be different than it had been in earlier exercises; here it is to explode sharply. This is done in order to free the voice from the unnecessary tensions caused by the physical effort in the rest of the body. The main thing is for the actor to commit himself to the physical rhythms, and not to worry about what he is going to do next. In fact, the actor does not need to know what he is going to do. He tells himself, "Move," and whatever movement he makes is fine. The less related it is to a dance movement, the better. Then, he moves again. Thus the actor establishes a rhythm.

When the actor feels that he has committed himself to the physical energy, he explodes the sound, the first syllable of the word *happy:* "hap," not "haaaaaaaaaaap." The latter would mean that he has committed himself, but that the energy of the voice is related to the rhythm of the body, and the actor therefore is not in command of his vocal resources. He is simply doing what the physical rhythm dictates. The actor on the stage must often move quickly, yet speak slowly; or even more important, move slowly, yet speak quickly.

Although I had begun these song-and-dance exercises for the singers and dancers in my classes, I began to use them with the actors as well. They are a simple series of exercises that train the actor to break his verbal habits and to extend his ability to control his expressiveness.

There was one young lady who had been with me on and off for quite a while and seemed to be doing the work, but making insufficient progress. I could see that she was doing the right things — concentrating, etc. — but there seemed to be little reaction and response. She was one of the first actors to try the song-and-dance exercise. She was a cool, unperturbable person, never showing much emotion, never responding much to anything. Therefore it was to be expected that she would be able to do this exercise quite well. If she was as precise and as definite as she seemed to be, then the exercise should have been simple.

When she began the exercise, she did not have any emotional reaction or involuntary responses, as some of the other actors had had. Yet she had difficulty in performing the first part of the exercise — the song — and seemed to have difficulty in performing the rhythmic section with the addition of the sound. That seemed both odd and inexplicable. There could only be one possible conclusion. Even though I was unable to observe it, something obviously was going on inside that young lady that interfered with and interrupted her expression. Things were happening inside her that made it difficult for her to use her voice.

I realized that something could be going on in the individual without its being seen. If an actor seemed to be doing what he was supposed to be doing correctly, and yet there was no visible expression of it, the conclusion had always been that the actor had no talent. Now, I was suddenly presented with the possibility that an actor might possess talent — even unusual talent — although it might not be visible. Clearly this young actress was feeling a great deal of experience. What could I do? Were there means by which I could unlock human experience from the habits and patterns of nonexpression in order to satisfy the demands of stage art?

I turned out to be lucky.

The simple song-and-dance exercise, which had in the beginning permitted me to discover what was happening within a human being, was in fact the solution to the problem. When the actress practiced the exercise, as long as she continued making the effort to make the sound and trying to do what I asked her to do in the movement part, she did in time become responsive and more expressive.

As I continued to try this with other actors, they would gain awareness of what was taking place within them by the mere fact that they stood still and eliminated any involuntary nervous expression. The actor would also eliminate the habitual tensions in the vocal and verbal areas that interfered with the process of expression. He'd begin to be able to express himself more really and intensely. In the second part of the exercise — the work with spontaneous rather than preset rhythms — the actor developed a new personal dynamic capable of expressing the intensity of his reactions, which had previously been stifled. I discovered that difficulty in the third part of the exercise — adding exploding syllables of a song while continuing the rhythms — implied an inhibition in the actor's expressive manifestations. What to do about it? Just do the exercise. When the actor was able to achieve this expressiveness in the exercise, I found that he began to make equal progress in his scene work. I observed a fuller expressiveness in his acting. Therefore, by the evidence of my observations, I discovered, without quite comprehending why, that there was a definite correlation between what the actor was asked to accomplish in the song-and-dance exercise, and the results it led to in dealing with the problem of expression.

I was for a long time puzzled by the fact that such a difficult problem in expression could be corrected by such a simple exercise. I tried to discover the logic behind it. The story of Achilles' heel suggested the solution. Achilles supposedly could not be killed because his mother had immersed him in a magic potion at birth. However, since she had to hold him by the heel in order to do this, that was the one area which had not been immersed and in which he was vulnerable. In battle with the Trojans, Achilles was shot in the heel by a poison arrow and killed. By presenting the actor with a simple problem, we had created the Achilles heel, a vulnerable area where the problem could be unraveled. Had we chosen a more difficult task, the unraveling would have been too difficult to accomplish.

The point of the exercise is that whatever is happening must come through; and if nothing is happening, then that is what is expressed. It should be noted, so that there is no misunderstanding, that nothing needs to happen in the exercise. When nothing happens, that is fine. There is nothing wrong. When nothing happens and you are not impelled by the presence of the public to do more, that means your instrument is responding perfectly. When, on the other hand, sensations and impulses are stirred in the exercise, the actor must contact them. He must be permitted to express himself through the deliberate demands of the exercise, not by involuntary nervous movements, gestures, and reactions, which are a form of stifling the expression of what is occurring.

The exercises I have just described are the first stages of the actor's training. This training starts with the actor's work on himself. First he must have the ability to relax, to concentrate, to be able to sense and experience intensely. At the same time, he develops the external facets of his being. He must develop and strengthen the voice and body by eliminating the stifling grip of habit and the inhibiting factors of nonexpression encouraged by social conditioning.

The second stage in the actor's training is to develop the ability to carry out actions truthfully and logically. At the same time, the actor learns to respond and adjust to his partner, not simply in a mechanical way, but by actually trying to convince his partner by making sure his meaning is clear. This is accomplished by extensive work in improvisation.* Then the actor begins to use animal exercises to approach the problem of physical characterization. This teaches him to isolate and comprehend the creation of physical behavior different from his own. He then learns to discover the experiences which stimulate his most vivid emotional responses, and to create them by means of the process of emotional memory. The actor continues to practice these exercises, even as he moves into the next stage of his training.

Next the actor begins to work with scenes from plays. It is customary in approaching a scene to emphasize the actor's interpretation of a part, the idea of a character and the theme of the play. While these do become involved and are part of the actor's approach, they tend to remain intellectual concepts and do not actually help to create the actor's embodiment of a role. One can have brilliant theoretic, literary, critical, or philosophical concepts of a play and not be able to create a reality on stage. Thus, at this point in training, these scenes are not important as they relate to the play; rather, they offer the actor an opportunity to exercise his ability to maintain his training skills within set dramatic sequences. The actor is not at this point concerned with the interpretation of the play or of a

---

* A type of improvisation work is a process we call "gibberish." Gibberish involves saying what you mean in a nonsense language. This forces the actor to be clear about what he is saying; it forces his partner to actually seek to understand, rather than only listening for his cue.

particular kind of character, whether it be Hamle
Kowalski, Othello, Blanche DuBois, Lady Mac
Willy Loman. He is not yet an artist, he is a craftsm
he is learning to practice his craft.

Stanislavsky tried to develop an approach that would
lead the actor to concrete procedures and help him to use
his talent to achieve the desired believable and logical
behavior. Stanislavsky's formulation is contained in the
well-known questions the actor asks: Who are you? Where
are you? What are you doing here? When or under what
conditions or given circumstances does this take place?
And how? — meaning, Which adjustments affect your
behavior? Often those terms are interpreted intellectually
and lead to mental conclusions that do not motivate the
actor to act. To correct this intellectual approach, it is
necessary to understand what is taking place in each scene.
"What is taking place" is easily confused with the "plot,"
but the plot is not always equivalent to the event that is
taking place in the scene.

In my work with actors on finding the event of a
sequence, we often use short stories by Ernest Hemingway, Irwin Shaw, Dorothy Parker, Colette, or de Maupas-
sant because they are complete, self-contained, and usually
well-written units. They serve to train the actor's awareness
and understanding of a situation. The dialogue in a play
often contains elements that characters would never say
but convey necessary information to the audience. The
novelist or short-story writer can relegate this to his
descriptions. This makes the dialogue in a short story
more representative of what a character would really say.
I also find that the short-story material forces the actor to
really find out what he is talking about, not just what he is
saying; and to find out how that relates to what the scene
is all about.

Let's take an example of how this procedure works.

Ernest Hemingway wrote a story called "Hills Like White Elephants." In it an American couple find themselves at a Spanish inn located near a railroad station. It is never clear — nor is it important — whether they are married or not. They have no monetary problems and they seem to seek only pleasure and enjoyment out of life. She is on her way to have an abortion and obviously would prefer not to have it. He seems unwilling to accept anything else but the present state of their relationship. At the end of the story she seems to accede to having the abortion. That's the plot. Why should this story be titled "Hills Like White Elephants"? At the beginning of the scene, she makes some innocuous remark that the hills through the trees look like white elephants, and he responds that he has never seen one. She says, "Of course you wouldn't," and he responds, "Why, because you say I wouldn't?" They order some drinks and the argument resumes. After she agrees to his wishes and he takes the luggage to the nearby station, she is left alone in the inn. She has told him to come back and they will finish their drinks before embarking on the final lap of their journey to the doctor.

Actors usually play this scene as an argument as to whether she should or should not go through with the abortion. This is what the action indicates. When, however, we start asking some of the questions, Who? What? When?, and so forth, we begin to arrive at a greater realization of what is taking place, and even why it is entitled "Hills Like White Elephants." She is obviously more sensitive and more imaginative than he is. She has hoped that their relationship would be unified and consummated by the birth of a child. He has no appreciation for what she desires and is interested only in continuing a life of ease and pleasure: they travel around, they drink, they enjoy themselves. He is satisfied with that, whereas, in the comments she makes, it is clear that she isn't. The title is therefore an indication of her realization that there is a chasm between them which will never be bridged.

Thus, at the end of the scene, when the woman is left on stage, the actress is free at this moment not simply to sit and wait for his return, but to fill the moment with what Stanislavsky called a "star-pause." This is a moment when the actor, left alone on the stage, can reveal to the audience what is actually transpiring. It is equivalent to a cadenza in a concerto, in which the instrumentalist shows his special skill, improvising on the musical theme.

If the actors in this scene understand only what is being said and not what is actually happening, they cannot realistically enact the play. They can build the argument, but it will lead finally to no understanding other than that a quarrel has taken place between two people.

By discovering the situation and not simply the sequence of the plot, the actors begin to be able to define the characteristics of the two people: the sensitivity of the one as opposed to the lack of sensitivity and the hedonism of the other; the hopes of the woman as opposed to the satisfactions of the man. Although this helps to clarify who they are, it does not go far enough in establishing elements of character which actors have a tendency to forget. She is pregnant, it's a very hot day. She seems willing to try new drinks, yet doesn't really drink any of them. It is necessary for the actress to create the sense of heat and to motivate why, when she drinks, she responds negatively to the drink.*

It is important to stress that every good actor, whether he knows it or not, follows precisely the same intuitive procedure. Some actors who rely only on technical skill simply indicate those sensory realities suggesting the drink

---

* Too often actors work out analyses of the background of the character, where they come from, what they've done, etc., without gaining any knowledge which will lead them to behave in any way other than the words imply.

and the dislike of it. Actors trained in the way described above are able to create the sensation of the heat, of the taste, and of course the experience of a woman in turmoil facing a situation which must have emotional repercussions. This will be revealed fully only when the woman is left alone; she will disguise her feelings when he returns and asks her whether she feels better and she answers, "Yes, I feel fine." The literal meanings which actors give to those lines now assume quite different texture, or what can be called "subtext." Subtext is the real meaning of the line — a compound of both sensation and emotion. To come on stage in the proper attitude, actors would then have to know the "given circumstances" implied by both the dramatic events and the actual physical events that preceded their arrival.

When the actor gains some awareness of the event as contrasted to the plot of the scene, he can then begin to divide the scene into units of action. These actions are related to the dramatic situation as well as being fully attentive to the areas of sensory reality. The actions relate to the place, to the daily activities he would usually perform in this place, etc. The actor must be able to create not only the behavior, but the state of mind and the emotional experience of the character. Physical action is determined by the character's emotional state. When Stanislavsky was directing *Othello,* he outlined for the actor Leonidov, who was to play the part of Othello, a very clear and precise physical sequence and physical actions for a particular scene. Leonidov disagreed with this sequence and questioned it. Stanislavsky countered by saying, "Ah, but you must understand the state of mind of the character," and then went on to describe Othello at that particular moment.

A real problem for the actor is, How does he create that state of mind off stage in rehearsal? This is where the études, the improvisations, the sense and emotional memories have to be created in order for the actor to get the benefit of his knowledge or of the director's suggestions.

During the fifty or so years of my activity as an actor, director, and teacher, I have found that if an actor approaches a scene intellectually, it rarely leads to results on stage. He continues to think one thing and do another. Whereas when the actor approaches a scene in an effort to discover the actions of that scene — what are the "given circumstances" that he must prepare in advance before he arrives on the scene? what would he be doing there as a result of those conditions if the scene as written was never to take place?, etc. — he will inevitably be driven toward the logical actions, behavior, and adjustment of his character. If he knows how to create the proper sensory and emotional experiences which motivate and accompany the behavior of the character, he will then be accomplishing the primary task of the actor: to act — that is, to do something, whether it be psychological or physiological. He must utilize his entire capabilities and equipment to create a human being on the stage acting within the conditions set by the playwright.

Perhaps a few other examples may suggest what the actor has to look for, be aware of, and create in order to fulfill the requirements of a scene.

It has been my experience that when actors are working on some of the comic short plays of Chekhov and I ask them what they were trying to achieve, they will state their intense desire to make it funny. I ask them, "When you read the scene, was it funny?" Invariably they answer, "Yes." I explain to them that the author has done the work of creating a situation which is funny. All that remains for the actor is to create as fully as possible the reality of that situation. He does not need to be funny — but the result will be.

There is a short story by Dorothy Parker called "You Were Perfectly Fine." It offers an excellent example of the actor's need to deal with simple sensory reality, leaving the comic development to the author. The scene deals with a character who awakes late in the afternoon after a night on the town, still hung over, with no memory of what happened the night before. The girl he was with the previous night enters. There is no description of how the man responds to her, but he questions her as to whether anything happened the previous night. She answers that he was perfectly fine, nothing happened — except that he almost got into a fight, that he poured clam juice down somebody's back, that he thought the waiter was his brother, that when he finally left the place he fell on the ice, and that he then took her home in a taxi, asking the driver to drive around the park for a good deal of time. She's sure that he certainly must remember the last, beautiful, and wonderful episode. Not knowing what is coming and embarrassed to admit that he does not remember, he feigns remembrance. It then turns out that he had proclaimed his undying love and had asked her to marry him. It is at this discovery that he says simply, "I need a drink."

When this scene is played with simple indications, we have the activity of the man waking up, or the suggestion of the hangover. The girl comes in and has to try to busy herself without actually having anything to do. The scene is sometimes amusing but hardly funny. If, however, the actor can create the reality of the situation — the way in which an individual would awaken from a deep sleep with a hangover, the physical pain that later turns out to be motivated by his falling on the ice, the stupor of forgetfulness; if he can make each embarrassment the woman describes significant and meaningful to him by concentrating on the identity of the individual who was the butt of the prank; and, finally, if he can properly create the inner shock of being surprised to find that he's gotten into something he cannot find a way out of — then the results are hilarious. This should be contrasted to the woman's enjoyment of the recital of these incidents; for her they are links in the chain that lead to the startling and exhilarating conclusion that they are to be married. The more she behaves as if this place were hers and as if she has a reason and a right to help him, the more the scene builds toward its surprising conclusion. A director might of course come up with some unusual social vision or some extraordinary theatrical inventiveness; but the basic realities that we have already described would still have to be fulfilled if the director's idea or interpretation is to become visible on the stage.

It has become customary to assume that our approach is valid for contemporary plays because it creates an additional degree of reality and intensity that is not within the capacity of the actor who does not possess training in the Method. Conversely, many people feel that a different approach is necessary for comic plays or for the classics. An illustration of how comedy can be approached by our procedures may be seen in a Chekhov farce, *The Boor*.

The story is simple. The play opens with a woman seated all in black before a religious icon. She is mourning the death of her husband, who often betrayed her when he was alive; but she mourns him by removing herself from the world to prove what real devotion can be. There is a commotion in the corridor. The old servant tries to stop the stranger from entering, but he will not be stopped and invades the widow's privacy. The stranger explains that her husband owed him money, which he now needs in order to pay the mortgage on his land. He tried to find the money elsewhere but was unable to do so. He has arrived after an all-night drive, desperate and sorry that he must request the money. She agrees to give him the money, but she must wait for the overseer, who will be there in the morning. The man argues that he must have the money today. He behaves in a rude and boorish manner, which forces her to leave the room. The man is left alone in the room. He expresses his frustration but is nonetheless impressed with the beauty of the lady and her remarkable behavior toward an undeserving husband. Still, he tells himself he will not permit himself to be persuaded by a woman's guile. The widow returns only to find that he is adamant; he will stay there until he gets the money and he's not going to be put off. The argument grows, and she finally challenges him to a duel. He is infuriated, but impressed with her flair. She then confesses that she has never fought a duel and he must demonstrate to her how to hold a dueling pistol. He is overcome by her courage and beauty and declares that he will not fire his pistol. She can do so, but he will not budge. She becomes outraged by his obstinacy, but he throws himself at her feet and declares his love.

When actors approach this scene — I have seen this numerous times — they invariably are prepared for the argument. The scene develops roughly; after all, they reason, the man is supposed to be a "boor" and the situation develops in an amusing, almost vaudeville-like fashion. However, when the scene is approached with an emphasis on the physical and sensory realities, it becomes both funnier and more interesting. I encourage the actors to work on what happened before the scene started. With the actress I try to create the reality of the way in which someone would behave if she had gone through the mourning process suggested by the author. To create the sensation of sitting immobile for long hours, I do something as simple as forcing the actress to sit still for fifteen minutes without moving, concentrating on the photo of her husband and on a sensory or emotional experience comparable to the reality she feels toward the husband.

The actress develops the necessary rhythm of speech, movement, and expression that would be the result of the circumstances described by the author. I encourage the actress to try to maintain this attitude and not to anticipate the quarrel. Thus she presents to the stranger an ideal image of the bereaved and devoted wife, who only gradually reveals her simmering feelings toward the scandalous behavior of her husband.

I follow the same line of preparation for the actor. It is described that he had been traveling most of the night and tried to catch some sleep lying next to a barrel of liquor in an inn. We help him to create the sensory reality that would lead to his being both physically tired and mentally distraught. He must create a sense of desperation. While he is rough in his behavior, he has been a soldier and an officer. I advise him not to anticipate the plot of the play. Thus, after he enters the room, the actor's natural tendency is to start talking. He has memorized the speech he wants to make to the widow and is ready to deliver it. But he has just created a commotion; the room is dark, and the only light is the holy lamp in front of the icon. The woman is dressed in black; her face is veiled. To stimulate the actor's awareness of the reality of the situation, I often either hide the actress or have her off stage when the actor enters. This way he has to be impressed both with the room and its strange atmosphere, and he cannot be quite certain of what object is in the chair. This leads to behavior both more unexpected and more startling than his precipitous entrance. He is respectful toward the icon and uncertain as to whom he is addressing. She shows no sign of being disturbed. She decently and graciously promises to repay the money. He responds joyously, only to be completely stunned by her inability to do so immediately. Concerned only with her own inner concentration and without any desire to create a scene, she logically insists that she doesn't have the money today; it will be available tomorrow. She tearfully expresses some of her feelings about her husband. In rehearsal, on one particular occasion, the actor playing the man couldn't stand to see a woman in such distress, and therefore a strange sentimentality in the character was revealed. At the same time, his desperation drove him to behave with the necessary rudeness and disrespect. Already the scene is prepared for a rather strange comic situation that contains within itself the possibilities of the ultimate conclusion.

This emphasis on the simple physical logic and sensory reality continues throughout the scene. When the woman leaves the room, the man is left alone, frustrated and desperate. He is at the same time tired and sinks into the chair, trying to keep from falling asleep. When the woman reenters the room, he has to struggle to his feet. He still has the manners of a former cavalry officer, but his desperation drives him to the crude behavior demanded by the situation.

In the scene where he shows her how to handle the dueling pistol, the physical logic dictated by his closeness to her excites his growing passion. The humor is heightened by the need to place her arms in the proper dueling position without encountering other more suggestive areas of her body. The author's structure is permitted to develop, with the actors filling in the necessary physical, sensory, and emotional constituents which help to bring the author's construction alive. The author does not want the actors just to act the quarrel and boorish behavior; they must create the moment-to-moment reality which motivates the lines. The actors make the author's dialogue not from the structure of the plot, but from the characters' immediate behavior. Thus, the reality allows the comedy to be expressed.

An example of a classic scene that gains immeasurably from this procedure is Juliet's potion scene from Shakespeare's *Romeo and Juliet*. This is a favorite scene for all actresses, yet it is astonishing how little logic and meaning has been brought to bear upon it.

The very appellation "the potion scene" is in itself indicative of the conventional approach to this scene. It is always acted as if the actress were committing suicide. The last part of the play becomes anticlimactic: Juliet dies, or seems to have died long before the scene in the tomb. But on examination, we find that though the scene has elements of the growing confusion and terror of a young girl forced to perform this dismal act alone, this conventional approach does not properly suggest the other elements of the situation. Juliet certainly has no intention of committing suicide; she is embarking on a dangerous and exciting act by means of which she will join her beloved. She is certainly closer to a girl who is eloping than to a girl behaving as if she were taking poison. The feeling that motivates Juliet is one of excitement and danger.

Juliet cannot share her excitement with the Nurse, who knows nothing about her plan; therefore, she can't wait for her to leave. When she does, Juliet is both relieved and elated. She can now proceed to carry out her exciting adventure. This is a young girl on her way to meet her lover. When she is left alone she doesn't know whether she will ever see the Nurse again. Juliet is thinking only of the separation from her family and of the banishment of her beloved when she complains of or expresses "a faint cold fear." This is not yet the fear of dying, but the natural fear of any dangerous, exciting deed.

When Juliet decides to call the Nurse back, she usually does so in a tone that clearly indicates that the actress knows the rest of the play and knows that the Nurse will not return. If the actress calls in a loud enough voice fearing that the Nurse will not hear her, it creates for the audience a sense of reality. It seems as if the Nurse truly might reenter.

Juliet takes the vial — the means by which she will accomplish her adventure — from its hiding place. As she is ready to take the potion and begins to imagine the possible consequences, she doesn't think of dying, but of awakening in the tomb with the bones of her ancestors scattered about. It is this thought that alarms her. The apex of her imagining is that she suddenly thinks she sees Tybalt. The actress is usually forced to stand or kneel on the stage, staring into space. Some logical motivation — the light, the movement of a curtain — must be utilized to make it seem possible for the young girl to imagine this apparition. She struggles with this belief and calls out: "stay, Tybalt, stay!" Then Juliet realizes that there is no apparition and that her fears, therefore, are groundless; she will then take the potion in a more logical manner. She will realize that she has let her imagination run away with her and return to her initial resolve and take the potion. For its proper execution, this scene demands the use of emotional memory.

Verdi, who was a dramatist in music, would at a moment like this usually put in an Ave Maria. There is no reason why the actress might not at the beginning of a scene investigate the normal behavior of a girl going to bed and saying her prayers. In fact, this might serve to help her to make a transition to the fears which ultimately overwhelm her, only to return at the end with a renewed faith in her act.

What I have described is not necessarily the only possible behavior in this scene. Nonetheless, it helps to suggest that a search for the reality of the situation and the behavior of the character leads to a more interesting solution for both the scene and the play than is supplied by the conventional approach.

My descriptions in these various scenes are intended only as illustrations to clarify the way in which all that has been achieved in the process of the training of the actor is of direct use in the process of acting.

The analytic part of the actor's work is, of course, essential to the actor's development as an artist. But Stanislavsky sought to replace the actor's mental, intellectual, and theorizing activities with truthfulness, experience, and behavior. He did this in order to make sure that it would not result in only verbal, mental, or formalized theatrical behavior that relates more to the director's ideas than to the actor's execution.

Some directors talk vaguely and philosophically of the truth of the play, or of the author's truth, when what they mean is nothing more than their own interpretation of the play. The actor's truth is first and last the truth of experience, of behavior, and of expression! The choice of the particular truth to be created derives from one's interpretation of the play. But the correct interpretation of a play in no way guarantees the truthfulness of the performance unless the actor is capable of convincingly creating the necessary reality intended to expose and to reveal the idea of the play.

Many who train actors are so immediately concerned with their interpretation of a play that they never really train actors, they simply coach them. The actors never learn to be creative. Actors who have been trained in the procedures outlined above can create a reality on stage and still adhere to the demands of the play. They can also make adjustments set forth by the director and still maintain truthfulness. That is why Peter Brook, a director who constantly searches for a heightened style of production, has expressed his satisfaction with working with so-called Method actors, because he can make the necessary demands on them and they are trained to execute them on their own.

THE METHOD AND
NONREALISTIC STYLES
Artaud, Grotowski, and Brecht

THE continuation and consolidation of Stanislavsky's and Vakhtangov's discoveries became the basis of the Method. To these we added further discoveries in the area of the actor's expressiveness. Certainly one of the most important aspects of the Method concerns its universal approach to the actor's problem and, at the same time, its flexibility. For instance, a widely reported criticism of the Method — and indirectly of Stanislavsky's training ideas — is its utter dependence on realistic texts and styles of performance. Or put another way, a Strasberg-trained actor can play Chekhov, Odets, and Miller, but not Shakespeare, Williams, or Albee. This line of reasoning probably developed from a viewing of the Group Theatre's play selections rather than from any deep understanding of its actor training. This criticism also ignores Vakhtangov's powerful influences on the Method's evolution.

Stanislavsky's work, interpreted in the light of Stanislavsky's achievement, can appear to be limited to the realistic style. Even Stanislavsky's efforts in the realm of elevated style or fantasy would tend to strengthen that opinion. On the other hand, Vakhtangov's equally valiant and brilliant use of the same procedures was inspired by a theatrical vision which he called "fantastic realism." In two epic productions, Vakhtangov demonstrated a range of styles: *The Dybbuk* was characterized by a grotesque mysticism, and *Turandot* was fancifully theatrical.

The work of the Group Theatre is significant precisely because it proved the group was able to apply the procedures of its actor training and arrive at different theatrical results — in our case, in plays that ranged from a new thirties' realism to sharp musical satire, such as *Johnny Johnson*.

The continuation of the Group Theatre's work into the Method seems to me to form the first concrete foundation for the training of what has previously been called the actor's imagination.

In the sixties, various experimental theories and achievements arose, whose "spectacular results," in the words of a highly enthusiastic observer, "threatened to smash a naturalism that directors from Stanislavsky to Lee Strasberg had for years inculcated in their actors."

In an article entitled "At the Grave of Stanislavsky," published in *Show Magazine*, Paul Scofield, a fine and distinguished actor, who starred in *A Man for All Seasons*, stated that unlike the "Method people," he preferred technique to spontaneous emotion. "They have to be lucky to hit the bull's-eye without technique. What happens to them on an off night? . . . They have nothing to fill the vacuum with." Obviously, Mr. Scofield was referring to his own experience in which at times the presence of spontaneous emotion led to magnificent results, while at other times his performance remained dependent on what he preferred to think of as technique. It should be clear by now that the basic problem of the actor's craft is the unreliability of spontaneous emotion.

More recently, Laurence Olivier stated that acting takes great discipline.

> I'm not a Method actor, though I've found Stanislavsky useful. Still it's not the whole answer. I do think this training would be wonderful for film actors, as the camera zeros in and captures two people being real together. But the problem in the theatre is being real fifty yards away. And that involves technique and skill — unfashionable terms these days. No art is simply a matter of talent.

Quite obviously, a technique which is unrelated to talent but simply deals with projection and skill is not art but remains only that, technique and skill. There is in Olivier's most distinguished performances more than just technique and skill. It is precisely this quality that the Method tries to define, to make conscious, to strengthen, and to exercise.

It is, however, the directors Artaud, Grotowski, and Brecht whose nonrealistic work seemed to displace the achievements of Stanislavsky and those who represented the intention of the Method. At the present moment it would seem as if the tide has turned again; the promises and expectations that were hoped for from their avant-garde approaches have not materialized.

Antoine Artaud's influence as a theoretician is widely proclaimed, but even his supporters are aware that none of his actual work demonstrated the effectiveness of his ideas. Many of his production plans are impractical.

The actor's training I have tried to outline above deals with the actor's expressiveness in a variety of styles. It is related to the concrete and real problems faced by the actor. Artaud outlined an approach to expressiveness in his "First Manifesto of the Theatre of Cruelty":

> Every spectacle will contain a physical and objective element, perceptible to all. Cries, groans, apparitions, surprises, theatricalities of all kinds, magic beauty of costumes taken from certain ritual models; resplendent lighting, incantational beauty of voices, the charms of harmony, rare notes of music, colors of objects, physical rhythm of movements whose crescendo and decrescendo will accord exactly with the pulsation of movement familiar to everyone, concrete appearances of new and surprising objects, masks, effigies several yards high, sudden changes of light, the physical action play of light which arouses sensation of heat and cold, etc.

Artaud does not seem very original in enumerating these means. Many of them had already been proposed by Edward Gordon Craig.

I share Artaud's feelings for the color, sight, and sound of Oriental theatre. However, I recognize that these aspects are historically related to social — often feudal — and religious conditions that have vanished and will not be revived. The fact is that these theatres are searching and looking for help in our Western theatres, without which they cannot find the proper representation of their own modern life. In art it is marvelous to be able to retain the master works of the past, but life goes on. If one wishes to return to some mystical womb, I understand and sympathize with the eternal need for security. But I share in and must continue to deal with the life that we live today, its struggle and its reality.

Jerzy Grotowski, the contemporary Polish director and theoretician, of course is different from Artaud. While others have felt that he was influenced by Artaud, Grotowski himself seems to deny that and has criticized Artaud's results. He feels that Artaud's effort to find the language of the body leads to mechanical clichés.

Grotowski is not just a theorist, but is able to put his theories into practice. Theatre for him has not been a medium of art, but seems to be a substitute for life. Recently, he has become more of a seer and seems to promote anti-theatre. In one of his recent lectures in New York, he advised young actors not to learn how to act, but to learn how to live.

Grotowski started by "worshiping Stanislavsky." He feels that Stanislavsky asked the right questions but gave the wrong answers. He is, however, critical of emotional memory and believes that it has led to "hypocrisy and hysteria."

It should be pointed out that Grotowski never saw the Stanislavsky productions which excited us in the twenties. I do not understand where he could have observed the "hypocrisy and hysteria" he speaks of. There was certainly no hysteria in any of the productions which the whole world witnessed. There was throughout Stanislavsky's writings a tendency toward idealistic, and therefore generalized, explanations. It was certainly much less than the mystic intellectualism of Grotowski. As I have tried to describe, Stanislavsky's technique of recall is valuable and useful because of its precision; it does not rely on some hypothetical "collective unconscious," as Grotowski's does.

There can be nothing but respect and appreciation for the enormous discipline involved in Grotowski's training of the actor. The actor is initiated into what amounts to a religious order or cult. Influenced by his Polish Catholic background, Grotowski visualizes the actor's process in almost "sacred" terms.

His exercises are divided into two basic categories. The

"corporeals" are a series of sharp, acrobaticlike head-stands, handstands, shoulderstands, and high jumps, done rapidly, continuously, and frenetically. The "cat," the basic corporeal exercise, is designed primarily for energy and the suppleness of the vertebrae. Actors get on all fours and stretch their bodies to resemble the cat in its various attitudes and positions. The "plastiques" are fast back-and-forth rotations of the joints: neck, shoulders, elbows, wrists, hands, fingers, hips, torso; also exercises of joints going in opposite or contradictory directions — the head going one way, the shoulders another, for example.

There is nothing wrong with exercises of this kind; they certainly do help to train the actor's instrument, and there are certainly many other forms of physical training which do the same. But for Grotowski these exercises are not for the purpose of physical development. They lead one to find one's "biological impulse." During the process, the actor supposedly discovers his physical impulses, together with his unconscious, mythic, or archetypal roots, which, in Grotowski's canon, are the basis for true creativity. This helps the actor toward the construction of a personal "psycho-analytic language of sounds and gestures" which are as unique to, and expressive of, the actor as is the self-contained language of words created by a great poet. The actor must, according to Grotowski, analyze "the hand's reflex during a psychic process and its successive development through shoulder, elbow, wrist and fingers in order to decide how each phase can be expressed through a sign, an ideogram."

I was one of the fortunate few privileged to attend the performances of Grotowski's Polish Laboratory Theatre in its United States debut in 1969. I had followed with interest and growing anticipation the reactions from abroad and the enthusiastic reports of young theatre artists like Andre Gregory. I was somewhat uneasy about the mystic nature of Grotowski's theories and his reliance on collective and mythic unconscious. However, I looked forward with great interest and concern to the results actually achieved, which I could not visualize from the descriptions in the reviews of the performances or from the descriptions of the exercises. On viewing the performance, I had the experience of sharing a special event. Instead of being seated when you arrived, you waited in the lobby. I was told the actors were preparing. (In some instances performances would be called off because the actors felt inadequately prepared.) The doors were opened and the audience, which had been waiting, all entered at the same time. I was immediately impressed with the dedication and the training of the actors, but unfortunately I was disappointed by the results. I had expected to see a mythic and transcendental experience and expression. Instead, it seemed to me that the gestures and movements were not expressive of a deep personal commitment, reaching toward a fresh, spontaneous, individual image or language; they were theatrically conventional. I was surprised and somewhat startled to discover that I could anticipate which actor was going to move and how.

In our work we call this "general emotion," as distinct from real emotion; that is, there is an indication of emotion created by an exertion of physical effort of the voice and body. The actor's experience of the energy that he is expending is often confused with the presence of actual emotion. A real emotion is easy and spontaneous and possesses little physical effort, though a lot of inner biochemical propulsion.

The use of the voice was an outstanding feature of the Polish Laboratory Theatre: the actors seemed able to use their voices in a way that would have strained those of many other actors. The method that Grotowski uses in training the voice deserves special attention, but the actual expression seemed to follow the conventional theatrical intonation. The voice followed a steady climb toward a point of emphasis. It captured a general sound image, but had none of the spontaneity and variety that reflects the possibilities of human expressiveness. There seemed nothing here to resemble the kind of remarkable ease and simplicity of the psychological gesture of a Duse, the emotional vividness and flair of a Giovanni Grasso, the extraordinary rhythmic aliveness of a Michael Chekhov, the beauty and voice of a Vassily Katchalov, or the pure musicality of the voice of an Alexander Moissi. These are, of course, high exemplars, but they are what every actor should aim at, what the basic problem of the actor's training should lead toward, and what is within the capacity of every actor to attain.

It has been explained that "the most important key to Grotowski's acting technique is impulse." And Grotowski has methodically and painstakingly searched for the source of impulse. Taking up where Stanislavsky left off, Grotowski asks certain questions: What is impulse? What leads to a particular gesture? What compels the actors to cry or howl, to speak softly or loudly, to move, to walk or run? How can impulses be replenished, recorded, and repeated? These are questions that every method of actor training must deal with, but Grotowski's basic assumption that only physical stimuli will solve these problems hides a mystical nature of his approach. The path from what Grotowski called "poor theatre," which emphasized the primacy of the actor's creativity, to his present attitude of "anti-theatre" mirrors his true intentions.

When I met Grotowski, in an effort to clarify what I was perhaps missing, I asked him, "Where are you going?" He answered, "I don't know." The answer turned out to be a prophetic reflection of his state of mind. For me, what we aim to express in the theatre remains an individual search.

After witnessing the performances of Grotowski's Polish Laboratory Theatre, I was, unfortunately, forced to agree with the conclusion of the critic Walter Kerr "that if it was mime, it was not sufficiently good mime, if it was dance, it was not particularly brilliant dance, and if it was acting, it was not good enough acting."

This criticism does not eliminate whatever value one may find in Grotowski's ideas about theatre or the stimulus one may find toward a search for new forms of a theatrical production. But it does relate to the basic problem of the actor's creativity and training. I do not wish in any way to downgrade the general historical value of Grotowski's work in the chronology of innovative developments in the theatre. I can only evaluate his contributions in relation to the specific problems we are dealing with.

The central opposition to the Method that is exemplified by these "external" or "objective" schools of acting is based on the scientific investigations of the psychologists William James and C. G. Lange. Meyerhold was among the first, in 1921, to counter Stanislavsky's training in affective memory with an external technique, called "biomechanics," that found its inspiration in the James-Lange Theory. Other directors followed suit, and today Grotowski is probably considered the leading theatre proponent of this external or objective psychological school. Essentially, the James-Lange Theory links muscular response with the sensation of emotion. Hence James's credo, "I saw a bear. I ran. I became afraid." Like Diderot's foundations, the James-Lange Theory, I feel, needs further analysis.

My first exposure to the James-Lange Theory of Emotion came from secondary descriptions in textbooks. These sources indicated that contrary to the general concept that "a person sees a bear (perception), becomes afraid (emotion), and runs (action)," James and Lange had discovered a different sequence. They believed that a person would perceive an emotion-producing situation, act, and then interpret behavioral and psychological responses to be a particular emotion. "The person who saw the bear would run, perceive himself running, become aware of the fact that he was afraid." This has become the foundation for most of the physical or external approaches to acting. These approaches negate the presence of an emotional experience and instead emphasize physical action as being either indicative of or leading to an emotional experience. This has led to declarations by Grotowski that "bodily activity comes first, then vocal expression. . . . First you bang on the table and afterwards you shout."

I had no reason to question the correctness of the description of the James-Lange Theory. However, as part of the process of checking some statements, I decided to look into James's own version of his theory. I was shocked to discover that his description was completely different in emphasis. In addition, it constituted a clear and precise statement of the "emotional" point of view. James's effort was directed against a spiritual and, what he considered to be, a vague and inadequate concept of emotion. James therefore emphasized that emotion consisted of clearly perceivable bodily acts. Unfortunately, the image of "running" was singled out of his much more precise description. James clearly stated in his *Principles of Psychology*,

Objects of rage, love, fear, etc., not only prompt a man to outward deeds, but provoke characteristic alterations in his attitude and visage, and affect his breathing, circulation and other organic functions in specific ways. When the outward deeds are inhibited these latter emotional expressions still remain, and we read the anger in the face, though the blow may not be struck, and the fear betrays itself in the voice and color, though one may suppress all other sign.

James himself came close to misstating his own hypothesis by declaring, "the more rational statement is that we feel sorry because we cry, angry because we strike, afraid because we tremble, and not that we cry, strike, or tremble, because we are sorry, angry, or fearful." These bodily states, however, merely help us to understand our emotions. James goes on to talk about how complicated emotional experience is and how individual the expression of an emotion is.

James expressed this as clearly as I have ever seen it formulated. The physical changes that are executed by a stimulus

> are so indefinitely numerous and subtle that the entire organism may be called a sounding-board, which every change of consciousness, however slight, may reverberate. The various permutations and combinations of which these organic activities are susceptible make it abstractly possible that no shade of emotion, however slight, should be without a *bodily* reverberation as unique, when taken in its totality, as in the mental mood itself. *The immense number of parts modified in each emotion is what makes it so difficult for us to reproduce in cold blood the total and integral expression of any one of them. We may catch the trick with the voluntary muscles, but fail with the skin, glands, heart, and other viscera.* Just as an artificially imitated sneeze lacks something of the reality, so the attempt to imitate an emotion in the absence of its normal instigating cause is apt to be rather "hollow." *(Strasberg's emphasis)*

I have never seen a better definition, description, or explanation of the difference between the "emotional" and the "anti-emotional" points of view in acting. The exercises in emotional memory, etc., are designed precisely to recreate an emotional state that can lead to expressiveness. And if this were not enough to prove my point, James continues:

> What kind of an emotion of fear would be left if the feeling neither of quickened heart-beats nor of shallow breathing, neither of trembling lips nor of weakened limbs, neither of goose-flesh nor of visceral stirrings, were present, it is quite impossible for me to think. Can one fancy the state of rage and picture no ebullition in the chest, no flushing of the face, no dilation of the nostrils, no clenching of the teeth, no impulse to vigorous action, but in their stead limp muscles, calm breathing, and a placid face?

An actor incapable of recreating the emotional feeling, unable to feel anything in the chest or to make his face flush other than by extreme physical exertion, must necessarily end up by dilating his nostrils, clenching his teeth, and tensing the voice to suggest the existence of something that is not present. James unequivocally declared that "emotion dissociated from all *bodily feeling* is inconceivable . . . our emotions must always be *inwardly* what they are, whatever be the physiological ground of their apparition." James expressed distrust in classification and description of emotions. He believed that questions such as What is the "real" or "typical" expression of anger or fear? have no objective meaning at all, and that "the moment the genesis of an emotion is accounted for . . . we immediately see why there is no limit to the number of possible different emotions which may exist."

Quoting from Lange, James wrote,

We have seen fright drive the blood into the head of its victim, instead of making him pale; we have seen grief run restlessly about lamenting, instead of sitting bowed down and mute; etc., etc., and this naturally enough, for one and the same cause can work differently on different men's blood vessels.

Dealing with matters that directly relate to the acting problem, he suggested that

an emotional temperament on the one hand, and a lively imagination for objects and circumstances on the other, are thus the conditions, necessary and sufficient, for an abundant emotional life. No matter how emotional the temperament may be, if the imagination be poor, the occasions for touching off the emotional trains will fail to be realized, and the life will be *pro tanto* cold and dry.

He believed that

as with instincts, so with emotions, the mere memory or imagination of the object may suffice to liberate the excitement. One may get angrier in thinking over one's insult than at the moment of receiving it; and we melt more for a mother who is dead than we ever did when she was living.

James then declared that the term "*object* of emotion" could mean both one which is "physically present or one which is merely thought of." "The revivability in memory of the emotions . . . is very small. We can remember that we underwent grief or rapture, but not just how the grief or rapture felt."

This is precisely the area that the exercises in our

training deal with in the effort to strengthen the capacity not just to remember, but to revive, that is, to relive, the emotion. This is much more valuable from the acting point of view.

Perhaps the awareness of the actor's problem makes me sensitive to statements by James and Lange which others have not sufficiently recognized or noticed. I quoted them at length here because it is important to recognize their relationship to my work.

The contributions of Bertolt Brecht seem to me on a different level than those of Artaud and Grotowski. Artaud's influence lies mainly in the realm of his ideas as circulated within a select critical fraternity. The ideas of Grotowski have been expressed in concrete productions that have, however, remained unknown to the general theatre-going public. The plays of Brecht, while they often represent political ideas opposing or challenging those of the audience, have nonetheless achieved a wide popular appeal.

Brecht's productions with the Berliner Ensemble seem to me to represent some of the outstanding theatrical contributions of the postwar period, not so much because of the dramatic ideas of the plays, but because of the superb theatricality and imaginativeness of his productions coupled with a simplicity, earthiness, and directness of acting. In fact, whenever the productions of Brecht reached the outside world, the general reaction of the audience was, "But we thought Brecht was supposed to be cold, intellectual, alienated, unemotional. This is exciting, colorful, enjoyable, and moving!"

Brecht's ideas seem to me to deal with the question of how an actor can express himself in a heightened theatrical style. Although Brecht's work is often thought of as countering Stanislavsky and the Method, he applied many of the same principles of truth and believability.

I happened to be in London in 1956 when the Berliner Ensemble first came to England (this was just after Brecht's sudden death); I can testify to the surprise and pleasure of both the audience and critics — feelings I shared. But I was not *as* surprised, because on the basis of my own experience with Brecht (which I will later describe), I had always felt that many of his followers had presented his ideas in an abstract, intellectualized, and analytic guise. This approach was an injustice to the immediacy, coarseness, and sometimes deliberate vulgarity which make his poetic writing so personally dynamic, and at the same time so difficult.

A general misunderstanding of Brecht's work led to the assumption that Brecht was opposed to Stanislavsky. There developed the perception of an abstract disagreement between the actor's art based on "experiencing" and that based on "demonstration" — hence the attribution to Brecht of coldness, negation of emotion, and formalism of production style.

Brecht himself became acutely aware of this misunderstanding. In a "Letter to an Actor" written in 1951, he expressed the realization that many of his remarks about the theatre were misunderstood, especially by those critics who purported to agree with him. He wrote: "I then feel as a mathematician would do if he read: Dear Sir, I am wholly of your opinion that two and two make five. I think that certain remarks are wrongly understood because there were important points which instead of defining I took for granted."

Brecht then responded to the question of whether acting is not turned into something purely technical and more or less inhuman by his insistence that the actor ought not to be completely transformed into the character portrayed, but should, as it were, stand alongside it, criticizing and approving. Brecht believed that this was not the case:

Such an impression must be due to my way of writing, which takes too much for granted. To hell with my way of writing. Of course, the stage of a realistic theatre must be peopled by live, three-dimensional, self-contradictory people, with all their passions, unconsidered utterances and actions. The stage is not a hothouse or a zoological museum full of stuffed animals. The actor has to be able to create such people (and if you could attend our productions, you would see them; and they succeed in being people because of our principles, not in spite of them!).

John Willett suggests that this is perhaps the most important of Brecht's modifications of his extreme theoretical position. I cannot quite agree with this. What Brecht was primarily concerned with was the same problem that Nemirovitch-Dantchenko and Vakhtangov had already drawn attention to. The actor must learn to differentiate between the reality and behavior he experiences and the reality and behavior of his character. The actor learns to create the necessary behavior, not mechanically and externally, but by stimulating his own reality to properly relate to that of the character in the scene. In fact, in his pragmatic essay called *A Short Organum for the Theatre* (1948), Brecht stated,

Even if empathy or self-identification with the character can be usefully indulged in at rehearsals . . . it has to be treated just as one of a number of methods of observation. It helps when rehearsing, for even though the contemporary theatre has applied it in an indiscriminate way it has nonetheless led to subtle delineation of personality. But it is the crudest form of empathy when the actor simply asks: what should

I be like if this is what were to happen to me? what would it be like if I were to say this and do that?

Brecht suggested that the actor should instead ask, "Have I ever heard somebody saying this and doing that?" It is obviously much simpler for the actor to ask himself, "When have I said something like this or done this?" Brecht even stressed what might be referred to as "the illusion of the first time" in acting when he admonished the actor that "along with his part he must commit to memory his first reactions, reserves, criticisms, shocks, so that they are not destroyed by being 'swallowed up' in the final version but are preserved and perceptible." He emphasized that "the learning process must be coordinated so that the actor learns as the other actors are learning and develops his character as they are developing theirs." Brecht constantly referred not only to what the actor has learned from his reading of the text, but how much more he then finds out about himself from the actual treatment which he gets at the hands of the other characters in a play during the process of rehearsal.

Brecht said that the actor's identification with the character is something to be avoided in performance. This is because Brecht feared that if the actor truly experiences, he is unable to deal with other facets demanded by the work on the character and the intentions of the scene. As we have shown, this is not the case.

Stanislavsky was dissatisfied with a particular scene involving a corrupt supervisor who insults people, steals from them, etc. In this scene the supervisor gets the drunken idea to dress himself and his companions as robbers in order to invade the forest and to frighten one of his friends. Since the part of the supervisor was played by the great Ivan Moskvin, the audience reacted with great sympathy and compassion to this scene. Stanislavsky tried to find ways to change the sympathy of the audience. He wanted to make them laugh at the actions, and still perceive the meanness and cruelty of them. He surrounded Moskvin's character with a mass of people who followed him like the tail of a comet, supported him, brought pillows, vodka, fifteen chairs, and other things. They were ordered to follow him at any cost, whether he was climbing in a tree or playing games on the ground. Thus the sympathetic trickster was disclosed as the cruel enslaver. Brecht witnessed this performance in Moscow and reported how the laughter froze in the throats of the audience. He called this a "completely dialectical performance" and laughingly added, "in the strictest sense, alienated."

One of Brecht's colleagues, Manfred Wekwerth, then described how Brecht was faced with the same problem in the production of *Mother Courage*. The performance in Zurich had shown how the public appreciated the vitality and indestructibility of Mother Courage. She mourned at the death of her children and blamed the war. The audience failed to realize that it is only by the participation of even small people, like Mother Courage, that war is possible. The audience failed to blame Mother Courage for the death of her children and for her inability to learn. For the production in Berlin, Brecht tried to discover how in those moments when the "mother" grieves, the "trader" in her persists. With the help of Helene Weigel, the actress playing Mother Courage, he found the answer. At the same time that the mother mourns the fate of her daughter and curses the war, she continues mechanically, as merchants usually do, to test with her fingers the flour that her daughter brought from the village. This scene was one of the most impressive of the entire play. It was difficult for the audience to empathize with the suffering of the mother without at the same time feeling indignation at the people like her who continued their dirty business with war. Wekwerth rightly pointed out that this example of Brecht's "alienation effect" in no way eliminated the truthfulness and reality of the scene and that this was completely consonant with Stanislavsky's ideas.

While Stanislavsky never used the word *alienation,* one of his suggestions to the actor was always to search for the opposite — never to be satisfied with the theatrical visualization of a character, but to discover the contrary elements which help to create the specific reality.

According to Wekwerth, the question as to whether the actor truly experiences or only demonstrates the reality is of little significance. Stanislavsky, he maintained, would never have presented any of his great actors with this "bureaucratic" question. But this is precisely where the problem of the actor's ability to express the reality of the actor's work on himself begins. Would another actress carrying out Brecht's intentions have achieved the impressiveness and conviction attained by the actress Helene Weigel? This essential problem — that it is the talent of the actor that determines his ability to create whatever reality he is faced with — remains fundamentally unsolved.

I'd like to add a note of personal confirmation about the relation of Brecht to the ideas of Stanislavsky and those of the Method. This has not previously been mentioned or described and may therefore be of some historical significance. Brecht's experience in America and his dissatisfaction with the productions of his plays has often been documented. In 1936 a number of the people in the Group Theatre approached me to work with them on one of Brecht's "learning plays." Since the problem intrigued me, I readily agreed. We met in my apartment, a large room over what was at that time the Al Jolson Theatre. Brecht was present at these rehearsals, sitting in the corner with his perennial cigar as protection; there was about him a strange abstraction and quietness which was like a coiled spring. The people sat around and started to read the play. I almost immediately stopped them. Somewhat diffidently, I ventured the opinion that this was not what Mr. Brecht wanted. They were not reading it in the way they would have approached it under the usual circumstances of a Group Theatre rehearsal, but with an effort to achieve what they presumably thought was the "alienation effect." I turned to Brecht for confirmation. He shook his head in agreement with me. I ventured the opinion that Mr. Brecht desired the actor to be real, truthful. He shook his head with intense confirmation. I explained that it was possible that Mr. Brecht did not wish the actor to be absorbed with the experience of that part at the moment, but that he desired the kind of reality that one has after something has happened and we describe it to someone. We are not at that time concerned with the emotional *intensity* of the event, but with the precise reality and truth of what has transpired.* Thus when I say, "I'm shocked," I permit the sensation of shock to be expressed, making no effort to act it out. I tried to suggest to the Group Theatre that what Brecht meant by distancing was a way of communicating a feeling to the audience without necessarily indulging in the same intensity of experience demanded in plays with a psychological emphasis. The

---

* I took this idea from Stanislavsky when he asked an actor to describe clearly what was happening in the scene. Speaking not as "he" but as "I," the actor described and acted out simply but truly: "I open the door — I am tired — it's dark — there's nobody here, I wonder where they went — I thought they would be home by now — I expected them to meet me — what time is it? — did I make a mistake?" The actor carried out the simple physical behavior that would accompany the sequence of this narrative process. The action did not remain simply thought spoken out, but was complemented by the behavior.

style of the play requires a different kind of expression, but the reality of feeling remains the same. Thus when I say, "I am angry," obviously I must sufficiently believe that I am angry, otherwise the expression will be neither real nor true, or as Brecht would put it, "natural."

Throughout my exposition, Mr. Brecht, who never uttered a word during the course of the rehearsals, kept indicating his approval by shaking his head in agreement with me. It was an interesting experience. I had felt that people misunderstood what Brecht desired. The "alien-ation effect" he talked of was not meant to deny reality. (This misunderstanding was not only behind the failure of many American productions of his work, but also the cause for Brecht's severe criticism of them.) I have always remembered the experience pleasantly and have therefore been steadfast in my belief that both adherents and detractors of Brecht misunderstood him.

In 1956, after Brecht's death, I flew to London to see the Berliner Ensemble production of *Coriolanus*. I had been concerned that the theatre would not be able to continue without Brecht's presence. I had followed its progress and was pleased with its ability to sustain itself. But I was especially interested to observe its handling of a Shake-spearean problem.

I was enormously impressed and stimulated by the production. Since I was a visiting American and the company was on a strict financial allowance, I invited a number of them for an after-theatre supper at one of the well-known establishments. I was particularly interested to hear how they had worked on the production and how they had arrived at some of the solutions through collective participation. Imagine my surprise, my hidden pleasure, when in describing to me how Brecht dealt with an actor having difficulty in a particular sequence, they told me about the narrative procedure that I had shared with Brecht during the course of the Group Theatre rehearsals he had attended. Unfortunately, those rehearsals had been terminated after a few weeks and no mention of them had ever been publicly made. Nor did I, at that time, have any evidence to corroborate my memory. A short while after my marriage to my wife, Anna, she was scouring the house, opening boxes to find what was in them — they had not been opened for years, and but for the tenacity of my late wife, Paula, they would have been lost — and she came to me with something she had found and asked me to identify it. It was a letter from Brecht in reference to this experience. This seemed to me to be the most direct indication of his positive reaction to both Stanislavsky and the Method. Brecht expressed his enthusiasm for our rehearsals and felt that we had been able to work very well together. He went on to describe the initial frustration he had felt when he tried to convey his sense of what was needed to save the American theatre. But in our group, he had found hope: he said that his time with us had shown him that a "revolutionary pedagogic theatre" was possible in America.

The work of Brecht remains for me probably the most significant from a theatrical point of view since Stanislavsky and Vakhtangov. The production by the Berliner Ensemble of *The Caucasian Chalk Circle* was the closest thing in style, imagination, and spirit to the productions by Vakhtangov of *The Dybbuk* and *Turandot*. There was a remarkable resemblance between Brecht and Vakhtangov, not only in their appreciation and attitude toward the work of Stanislavsky, but also in their search for additional means to emphasize and express the social and theatrical character, including the contours of a particular play. The productions of the Berliner Ensemble, especially *The Cau-*

casian Chalk Circle, remain among the half-dozen outstanding experiences of my life. But Brecht's "non-Aristotelian" theory of theatre is represented mainly in his playwriting; the best part of his work with actors derives from Stanislavsky and perhaps even uses the techniques of the Method.

IN CONCLUSION

C OMMON to both Stanislavsky's system and the Method is the central tenet of the creativity of the actor. The Method considers the actor as a creative artist who must translate the ideas, intentions, and words of the author into a living presentation. In this presentation, the sound of the word contains not only meaning, but sensation, emotion, and behavior. A new reality is achieved — related to the words, but often independent of the words. It might even be suggested that the Method accepts Gordon Craig's enunciation of the art of the theatre; but instead of demanding from the actor the clarity and precision of a "Super Marionette," it stresses the creativity of the actor as the central instrument by means of which the art of the theatre is achieved. The practical work of the Method has been so concrete and technically proficient, it tends to obscure the strong, intense, ideological base on which it rests. The results achieved are so well known it has been necessary to refer to its theoretical foundation for its corroboration.

The discoveries of Stanislavsky and their significance,

together with the perspective and experience provided by the Method, seem to me to provide for the first time a concrete foundation for the understanding of the actor's creativity, and thus, to provide the basis for the training of the actor. In addition, this foundation helps to clarify the problem of creativity in general, especially as applied to the other arts. But I would like to suggest that it may be of particular value on a much wider plane, not only to actors or artists, but to all human beings in their daily lives and in their search for fulfillment.

The world is agog today with all forms of psychophysical exercise: meditation, Zen, Yoga, the search for inner peace and relaxation. The scientific world is particularly concerned with the growing problem of mental and emotional stress. Stress arises from special pressures that build to an abnormal degree and interfere with the activity of the individual. While stress is experienced by a small percentage of the population, tension is something experienced by every human being. The difference between the two has not been sufficiently delineated.

Tension — not as mental or emotional disturbance, but as the generation of unnecessary energy that interferes with the normal functioning of the human being — is part of the natural state of living. Every human being, no matter what he may think, is subject to this continuous tension. The extent to which the ordinary individual is subject to what might be called normal tension is incalculable. While people are aware of moments of stress and disturbance, few individuals are ever conscious of the extent to which their activities are conditioned by "normal tension." In fact, they usually believe that they are relaxed even when they are making a deliberate effort to relax. They may seem relaxed, even to the practiced eye, but the nerves and muscles continue to tense automatically without the individual's awareness.

Procedures for simple relaxation, which I have described in this book, are something that every human being can take advantage of in his daily regimen. Everything that an individual does involves an expenditure of energy. Unnecessary energy serves to interrupt and interfere with the natural functioning of the human instrument and leads to many psychosomatic symptoms that do not necessarily result in mental or emotional disturbance. Every human being is subject to these natural tensions.

General education today is concerned with the training in memorized knowledge, often confused with intellectual pursuit. We are all well aware of people who have little academic background but whose intelligence is very high. We are equally aware of people whose memorized knowledge results in — as Clifford Odets once described it — "a mind of useless information." It seems to me that a good deal of the widespread student disturbances at colleges and universities a few years ago (and which still continue to "simmer") were the result not only of social and political differences of opinion, but were also based on the students' feeling that the knowledge that they were acquiring did not leave room for their individual experience, and therefore did not prepare them for the actual processes of living. Technical and scientific education has made great strides on a mass level, and that is essential for meeting the demands of our industrialized world. This kind of knowledge, however, tends to make people feel more and more like atoms — as mere cogs in an enormous wheel in which human will, desire, and feeling are irrelevant.

While the mental aspect is emphasized, the affective areas, the sensory and emotional areas, are left uncultivated to grow like weeds in a garden, rather than tended and nurtured for the full flowering of the human being. So negligible is this concern that terms like *affective memory*, *sense memory*, and especially *emotional memory* are hardly mentioned in scientific literature and have only recently begun to appear in the work of a few psychologists. The training of the senses and of the emotions should be an essential part of our educational system, and the procedures discovered for the training of the actor could prove to be of inestimable value in this regard.

An even greater problem remains unresolved in our educational system: the problem of communication. Our society has spent so much time and has achieved such startling results with the discovery of new mechanical processes of communication, but we have somehow forgotten that the process of living demands the ability to respond, to make contact, and to communicate one's experience to another human being. The problem of expression has been treated as a purely mechanical process, involving the voice, speech, rhetoric, rather than as a means of sharing one's individual way of experiencing. Only artists have managed to break through this vicious wall by using their special sensitivity and particular skill in communicating their experiences. All human beings are in even more need of this, if life is not to deteriorate into the "playing of games," which many psychologists, and even some theatre people, have discovered and proclaimed a way of life.

It is my firm belief that the discoveries and procedures essential for the actor's capacities are equally, if not more, necessary for the layman. This seems to me the great historical contribution of Stanislavsky, who always spoke of "the life of the human spirit," and the additional contribution made in our own country for these last fifty years or more by the practitioners of what is commonly referred to as "the Method."